Smart Kids, Stupid Choices

Dr. Kevin Leman

Smart Kids, Stupid Choices

A SURVIVAL GUIDE FOR PARENTS
OF TEENS. HELPING KIDS MAKE GOOD
DECISIONS ABOUT PEER PRESSURE,
CHOOSING FRIENDS, SEX, DRUGS,
DATING AND MORE...

Regal Books

A Division of GL Publications
Ventura, California, U.S.A.

Published by Regal Books
A Division of GL Publications
Ventura, California 93006
Printed in U.S.A.

Trade Edition, 1987

Library of Congress Cataloging-in-Publication Data

Leman, Kevin.
    Smart kids, stupid choices.

    Rev. ed. of: Smart girls don't and guys don't either.
    Includes bibliographical references.
    1. Adolescence. 2. Youth—Sexual behavior. 3. Adolescent psychology.
4. Parenting. 5. Dating (Social customs) I. Leman, Kevin. Smart girls don't
and guys don't either. II. Title.
HQ796.L366   1987   305.2'35   82-7686
ISBN 0-8307-1191-0

2 3 4 5 6 7 8 9 10 / 91 90 89 88

Rights for publishing this book in other languages are contracted by Gospel
Literature International (GLINT) foundation. GLINT also provides techni-
cal help for the adaptation, translation, and publishing of Bible study
resources and books in scores of languages worldwide. For further information, contact GLINT, Post Office Box 488, Rosemead, California 91770,
U.S.A., or the publisher.

Dedication

This book is affectionately dedicated to my dad and mom, John and May Leman, who persistently encouraged me, throughout my difficult adolescent years. More importantly, they had the courage to tell me what was right and wrong, and the wisdom to allow me to make the choice.

Acknowledgments

Thank you to Richard Kuykendall for his invaluable assistance in the research for this book.

Thank you to the many people whose encouragement, support and tireless contributions to the manuscript made this book possible.

And thank *you* for buying this book. Without people like you there wouldn't be any successful books or authors.

Contents

Introduction

Adolescence Isn't Terminal

I begin this book with the bit of good news above to encourage the many parents who are struggling with the mysteries of trying to guide their children through the most frightening, bewildering, exciting, chaotic time of their lives. What makes it doubly difficult is that all of this pressure squeezes teenagers when they are most vulnerable, during those years when they are quite capable of making mistakes that can leave permanent scars on their lives.

Parents hear plenty about those scars. We are so saturated with stories about the turmoils and tragedies of teenagers that we have come to believe that the problems of adolescence have been around since the beginning of time. This, of course, isn't true. According to an aptly titled article "Growing Up Too Late Too Soon," adolescence is a phenomena that did not appear until the last century. The term "adolescent" was unknown until the Industrial Revolution created societies where the age of economic independence and marriage is delayed past puberty.[1]

In other words, adolescence is a creation of culture, and that's the rub. Because our present culture forces children to go through the long period of dependency called adolescence, we have set them on a collision course with our own parental authority.

It is no wonder that parents struggle with getting through to teenagers to help them make smart decisions, when those same teenagers are not always interested in advice from their parents. Teenagers are well-known for loudly protesting that they are smart enough already. Furthermore, they tend to believe they are indestructible—way beyond needing any help from someone as ancient and outdated as a parent. Almost every week as I counsel I hear it from the young people themselves:

"Why bother talking to my parents? They're from another planet. It's hopeless."

"I should ask my dad for advice? How could he possibly know how I feel?"

"Look, I'm not a kid anymore. I can handle it."

Unfortunately, great numbers of teenagers don't "handle it" all that well; nonetheless, they still refuse to listen. As countless parents have told me:

"I can't understand it. We've put just about all of our time, blood, sweat, and tears into raising our kids, and now who do they listen to? Their friends. Or some rock star who should be locked up!"

Your Actions Can Outshout the Peer Group

No parents I know of have escaped the well-known

power of the peer group. Moms and dads of teenagers quickly discover that their children pay much more attention to the opinions and ideas of their schoolmates and friends than they do to what they hear at home. But there is an encouraging note in all of this. While teenagers seem to ignore what parents *say,* they carefully observe what parents *do.* Wise parents open their lives—not just their mouths—in order to communicate with their teenagers. Sad to say, a lot of parents try to cover up their blemishes—sort of like ostriches trying to hide by sticking their heads in the sand.

Such was the case with a mother who came with her 16-year-old son for counseling after he got in a great deal of trouble at school. We were making pretty good progress with the 16-year-old until the day he got stopped by a police officer who found an open bottle of wine in the back seat. The mother reacted with such rage that she was still visibly upset six days after the incident when they came to see me for their next appointment.

I met with both of them in my office, and things didn't go very well. At one point, her son asked her a direct question:

"Didn't you ever drink and drive at the same time?"

Mom shouted, "Of course I didn't!"

I had all I could do to stay on my counselor's chair. From prior sessions I knew this woman was an alcoholic. Surely she had driven while drinking at some point in her life.

I had her son leave the room for a few minutes, and then turned to her in disbelief and asked, "Do you mean to say that you never operated a car when you were drinking or drunk?"

She answered, "Of course I have. I've driven under

the influence several times. But I certainly didn't want him to know that."

What a tragic and foolish mistake this mother made. I hadn't been fooled by her lie and neither had her son. She had missed a golden opportunity to communicate with him at a level she had never reached before. If she'd had the courage to admit her mistakes she possibly could have helped him see how foolish it is to drink and drive. At the very least she could have established new feelings of empathy and communication between them.

But she chose to play the ostrich. She stuck her head in the sand, while her son and I saw her as she really was. I could make little progress with the boy after that session. He simply wasn't interested.

Share the Real You, Not the "Ideal"

My point is simple. If you are going to have any kind of communication with your teenagers, you must be willing to share your real self with them, not just the ideal self you would like to have them think you are. If you are going to enter the private world of your teenager you must be brave enough to be open and to relate some of the realities and complexities of your own life.

This is not easy. As you open up to your teenager you will have to go back to your own adolescent years and rekindle the thoughts, feelings and experiences you had while in junior high and high school. And if you are successful at rekindling those memories of teenage years, it is possible you can get very uptight with your own teenager. Why? Because you will fear that your child will make the same kinds of mistakes you made during adolescence! Parents often say to me in protest, "I can't admit to my teenager the things I did back in high school. This will just set a bad example, and give him the right to do the same things I did."

Nothing could be further from the truth. In fact, I have news for you, Mom and Dad. The jig was up long ago. Your children have known for years that you are not perfect. Everyone makes mistakes. The key to a family is to have the people who are close to you still love you— warts and all. You build that kind of love when you share your flaws openly with your children. They will not think less of you; on the contrary, they will be much more approachable and willing to listen to what you have to say.

I am often put on the spot as a counselor because people tend to think I have the answers to all of life's problems. One of the things I enjoy the most is going on radio and television talk shows to help husbands, wives and parents with their problems. On more than one occasion on national television I have admitted to a caller that I wasn't quite sure how to answer a particular question in the short time television provides.

I have had the same thing happen in seminars and workshops. I find that when I am brave enough to dig down deep into my own life and relate to the parents who have come to get help with tremendous burdens and anxieties, they in turn open up and pour out their hearts to me.

I have to admit, however, that it is tempting to play the role of expert on certain occasions. As a practicing psychologist and author of several books on parenthood and marriage, I am extremely sensitive to how people view me and my family. At times I have this overwhelming feeling that everyone thinks my children and my marriage ought to be perfect. Obviously, they are not. And if I tend to forget that from time to time, my wife and my children can bring me back to reality in a hurry.

My wife, Sande, is the sounding board in my life. Besides being everything I could ever want in a wife, she is my closest friend. And she keeps me humble and very honest.

For example, I had been gone on a speaking engagement one weekend and came home to find the water trickling down the street from our garden hose. Now, when I am gone for three days, I really miss Sande and the children. But one thing that can really make me angry is to have the children play with the hose in front of the house and let the water run, especially in the summer. (In Tucson, Arizona, where we live, water bills get high enough without letting the hose run down the street.)

So I stalked into the house. Were my first words full of joy and excitement because I had been reunited with my loved ones? Not quite. As I hit the hallway I roared, "Who left the water running in front of the house?"

From the kitchen came Sande's answer, "Oh, he's home, the family counselor."

It is strange how a few words from your wife can bring you down from your high horse (and your pedestal) in an instant. I put down my bags, went back outside and did the necessary thing. I turned off the hose.

I share that little story with you to illustrate that all families have their moments of tension, and anyone can have his times of imperfection and shortcoming, no matter what kinds of letters appear after his name. I am glad that to my children I am just "Daddy." I'm not a psychologist, or Dr. Leman, or a Ph.D. I am just Daddy, and I am quite capable of saying the wrong thing and hurting tender, budding teenage feelings by suggesting that a certain boy is special when my daughter would rather not talk about that just now.

As the father of one daughter well into the waters of adolescence and another daughter poised on the brink, as well as a son who will be there all too soon, I am learning new understandings of words like "I'm sorry," and "I was wrong." But if I am to help my own kids get through the turbulent, wild waters called adolescence, I must be willing to take the first step to enter their private world. That means establishing a spirit of cooperation and equality. By equality I don't mean that I have to deal with my children as their superior. I do have to deal with them as their parent, placed by God as an authority over them.

I believe parents can be in charge, but still allow their children to feel that spirit of equality that says they are important, that they can make smart decisions if we give them a chance.

So open up. Begin to allow your teenaged children to see who you really are. Then, and only then, can you help them with the tough subjects: peer pressure, dating and sex, love, saying no to alcohol and drugs. We will talk about all of these in the pages ahead, and I'll try to give you a few answers. I don't have all of the answers. Nobody does. But I do know the first rule: *be real.* Your kids will love you for it—and maybe, just maybe, they will even listen to what you have to say!

Chapter 1

Is There an Adolescent in the House?

If you were to ask most parents of teenagers what an adolescent is, they would probably not be too kind in their description. Many a parent has marveled at the great change his or her child undergoes as he becomes an adolescent. All of a sudden this kid who never got within six feet of a washrag in his whole life now stands before a mirror scrubbing his face until it glistens; he shampoos and blow-dries his hair at least once a day and sometimes more, seeking perfection. The adolescent daughter takes a bath and leaves the water running continuously—with the stopper still in—so the "schmootz" floating on the water runs out through the overflow drain instead of sticking to her body.

This excessive concern with their physical appearance is tremendously burdensome for many teenagers because it's during their adolescent years that they encounter all kinds of physical problems: skin blemishes, lack of coordination, tongue-tiedness, and a disturbing emerging sexual awareness. Research substantiates the fact that sex drive is probably the greatest during those late teenage years—16-18.

All of these seemingly negative factors contribute to the adolescent's self-esteem. It is critical that we as parents understand that the poorer a teenager's self-esteem is, the greater will be the impact others have on his value system. They become more susceptible and vulnerable to the thoughts, wishes and desires of others, especially those of their peers.

Adolescents Want to Be Perfect

Can you imagine a big zit on Madonna's face? Or Michael Jackson falling over a crack in the sidewalk?

It's no wonder adolescents don't have good feelings about themselves. Look at the models our world portrays to them—Tom Cruise, Michael Jackson and Madonna . . . with these examples is it any wonder that adolescents are critical of themselves and others? Teenagers are great flaw-pickers.

If an adolescent happens to be physically different—even in the least way—watch out. Things are going to get rough. And about the first sign that a kid is different is in the nickname other kids put on him.

Thinking about my own teenage years I remember some of the names we gave kids in my peer group—Moonhead, Jughead, Bellhead and Craterhead. I was Craterhead. I happen to have two chickenpox scars on my forehead and one of my "friends" thought that was sort of funny. One evening he branded me "Craterhead." I tried to laugh it off, but it hurt. To this day I have never forgotten that.

Adolescents are sensitive about their own differences, but they are critical and sometimes cruel to their peers who are different. I must admit that I was involved in giving the "girl with the flattest chest in the eighth grade" a pair of falsies for her thirteenth birthday. I flinch when I remember the young lady opening that gift at her party in front of all us kids. Most of the guys were gathered together in one corner laughing and screaming and having a great time at this 13-year-old's expense.

I remember the many times we used to choose ball teams, and as we "chose up" our teams, more often than not the same kid in our neighborhood was the last one to be picked. I'm surprised he came around as much as he did. After everyone else was chosen it always got down to, "And you can have Harold." After all, he did bring the ball and bat, which entitled him to play right field and bat ninth in our line-up.

How do you suppose teenagers get so sensitive to this whole area of being perfect? For one thing they're bombarded daily with perfect models proclaiming the virtues of various products—from skin cleansers to soda pop—on the boob tube. Not only that, but those of us who claim to be part of the adult society enforce perfectionism in our own children. Why do we think *our* kids have to be best at everything?

In addition to this aspect our whole perfectionistic society isn't very tolerant of mistakes. Even teachers who have been trained to be sensitive to children have the audacity to write at the top of the paper "-3." What's wrong with " + 47" at the top of a 50-word spelling test? You see, we've become a society of flaw-pickers.

Have you ever had the experience of sitting in church listening to a youngster play the flute or clarinet or in a school concert when suddenly the child hits a note that's never been recorded in all of musical history? What kind of feelings went through you when you heard that child make a mistake? Did your heart pound? Did you get very uncomfortable and clammy with embarrassment for the performer? And it wasn't even your kid! As a society we've become too good at thinking in terms of perfection and reinforcing perfectionistic notions in our children's minds.

Adolescents Feel Inferior

James Dobson said it best in his book *Preparing for Adolescence*. He refers to the "canyon of inferiority."[1] If there's one thing that characterizes adolescents it's that feeling of inferiority—that awkward feeling that says, Nobody else in the world is as ugly as I, as clumsy as I, has as many pimples as I, etc. Of course it doesn't help his adolescent ego when the 14-year-old male answers the phone and the person on the other end of the line says, "Hello, young lady, is your mother home?"

Probably the most common statement parents make about their teenager or young adolescent is that they just don't understand what has happened to their child. Just yesterday little Snooky was so sweet and cooperative and loving. Now she's irritable, cantankerous, volatile, and unpredictable.

I believe that self-esteem is probably at an all-time low during the adolescent period. When everything seems to be going wrong, when things seem to be piling up emotionally, many teenagers choose to strike out. And who is their target? Those who are the closest—moms, dads, brothers, sisters. Their thinking might be along the line of,

"OK, life is being unfair to me so I have a right to let somebody have it."

Why do most kids see themselves as being worth very little during their adolescent period? Prior to adolescence most of these kids were well adjusted, happy, good-natured, and helpful. But seemingly overnight they turn into something ugly, resentful, moody, and even disrespectful.

Many of these feelings, of course, are caused by the teenager's physical changes. But a great deal of the frustration teenagers suffer is caused by us, their parents. Most parents today, I feel, have done a beautiful job of snowplowing the roads for their children.

We think we know what's best for our children, and because we know what's best for them, we haven't given them enough decision-making opportunities. Many times during seminars around the country someone will stop me in midspeech and say, essentially, "Hold on! Now wait a minute. You've gone far enough. I think my wife and I know what's best for our children. And in our home we have rules and regulations and everyone must follow those rules and regulations regardless of how they feel."

After I've given the gentleman the opportunity to speak his mind I usually respond, "That's fine. But what I'm trying to point out is that if you don't give your child some freedom to make his own choices, you are setting him up for all kinds of problems. And when he faces the most important decisions of his life he may have a problem making the right choices." No parents can make those decisions for their children. It's the same thing in many other areas of their lives: children and adolescents must be given plenty of opportunities to decide for themselves—of course, with early parental guidance.

Ginny, age 17, was a beautiful young lady. Her blonde hair and blue eyes were accompanied by a beautiful figure and a neat, outgoing personality. To top it off, she was a cheerleader and student body officer. Everybody liked Ginny. By her own admission she was the only virgin on her high school cheerleading team. Yet she never lacked for male attention.

She was really blessed with a neat relationship with her mom. She could talk with her mother about everything. Frequently after a Friday or Saturday evening date, Ginny and Mom would stay up until after 2:00 A.M. talking about everything from that evening's date to some of the more debatable issues of our society.

One Friday afternoon Ginny came home and told her mother that she wanted to go to a party, a party "everybody" was going to. It was the biggest party of the school year. Ginny asked her mother to drop her off at the party. Because of their open relationship Ginny told her mom that she was a little concerned because there would probably be some smoking and drinking, and probably pot smoking as well. But it was a party that Ginny wanted very much to attend.

It would have been so easy for Ginny's mom to say, "You're not going to any party, young lady, where there's pot smoking, drinking and such going on. You're going to stay home." But she didn't. She did a very brave thing. She told Ginny that it was her decision, and if she wanted to go Mom would be happy to drop her off. In spite of her many reservations, Ginny still wanted to go. The pluses outweighed the minuses.

Mom dropped her off at the party and, as she did, she said, "Ginny, I'm going to be down the street about half a block. I'm going to wait there for 15 minutes. If things are not what you think they should be, feel free to come on out and I'll give you a ride home."

Well, you guessed it. Ten minutes later Ginny was in the car. "Mom, I couldn't handle it. No way! It was a zoo. There were a lot of older people there—kids from other schools and university students as well—drinking and smoking and acting crazy. I want to go home."

I often think of Ginny's mom—what a brave, wise and loving woman! She knew what was best for her daughter. It would have been very easy just to say no. But she gave her daughter the right to make the decision about the party. One of the reasons why Ginny's mom could give her that decision-making opportunity was because she had brought Ginny up in a home where, from the very beginning, Ginny was given choices. So although this was a more sophisticated choice than she had ever made before, she had plenty of practice as a youngster in making decisions.

Adolescents Want to Be Like Everybody Else

I think maybe one of the reasons Ginny was able to make such a wise choice where other adolescents might not is because her mother's confidence in her gave her the strength to be different, to resist going along with the crowd when she knew it was wrong.

Teenagers are under a lot of pressure to conform, to be like everyone else in their accepted peer group. I remember one 16-year-old who was in a department store. After selecting a shirt, paying for it and getting it wrapped, he asked the clerk, "Excuse me, if my parents like this shirt, can I return it?"

Teenagers seem to go out of their way to be "in"—

but "in" according to their peers' standards—not their parents'. In the early sixties if you were "in" your shirts were button-down shirts. Everything was button-down. One of my cousins watched his father leaving the house dressed in what we referred to as a "fly-away shirt," a shirt without button-down collars. The 15-year-old asked his father, "Are you going out of the house like that?"

A few years later no self-respecting teenager would be caught dead in a button-down shirt. They were no longer popular. Now the style has made a comeback. These fickle fads can mean life or death to the acceptance-seeking teenager.

What's interesting is that peer pressure seems to be highly evident not only in early adolescence, but in late adolescence as well. I worked for 14 years on the University of Arizona campus as Assistant Dean of Students in charge of code of conduct and discipline. I had a ball at registration time! Watching new students come into a university is an experience every parent ought to have. The first few days a freshman student can be spotted a mile away on campus. They're the ones wandering around in a stupor, looking up at the tall buildings, bumping into palm trees, asking stupid questions like, "Excuse me, but could you tell me where the TBA building is?" "TBA" means "to be announced" and it's found in the schedule of classes. It's a very typical question for a college freshman to ask.

But after a couple of weeks even those of us who claim to be experts in the area of students on campus find it very difficult to identify a freshman from the rest of the upper classmen. Why? Because freshman quickly learn to read what is expected of them by way of the peer group and blend in. Their dress, demeanor, language, even the way they walk is dictated by the peer group.

Peer pressure is alive and well even on a college campus where students are quick to point out how individualistic and free of family restraints they are.

Adolescents Are Sexually Aware

Sexual awareness and activity is a very natural part of adolescence. Most adolescents are woefully ill-prepared to deal with and comprehend the many changes that are occurring in their bodies. Many children are taught that sex is essentially bad, so they become confused when they experience, at adolescence, the first pleasurable feelings of sex. This may come as a result of self-stimulation or perhaps through fantasizing.

Ronald L. Koteskey, in the article, "Growing Up Too Late Too Soon," points out that parents must recognize the frustrations today's teenagers have. He says that during this "period of celibacy" parents need to recognize that (1) young people face sexual frustration not faced by people a century or more ago; (2) adolescence is a creation of culture; (3) orgasms while asleep and masturbation are likely to occur before marriage.[2]

That brings up another big thing that kids say "everybody's doing." I found that there are two words that many adults really can't handle very well. The first one is *sex*, and the other is *masturbation*. When either of these words is brought up in conversation many people will tune you out almost automatically. I found this true recently on a book tour. I was in Chicago and I called a bookstore to inquire as to whether or not my latest book, *Sex Begins in the Kitchen*, was in. A woman clerk answered the phone and I asked, "Do you have *Sex*

Begins in the Kitchen?" After a short pause this woman literally screamed into the phone, "Where I have sex is none of your business." She hung up on me. I must admit I didn't even have the courage to call her back. All she heard was the word *sex* and she drew an instant inference and tuned me out.

There are many reasons why we have tuned out the word *masturbation*. One reason is that the term itself comes from two latin words that mean "to pollute with the hand." It doesn't even sound like a nice thing to do, does it? But one thing you can pretty much count on is the fact that your adolescent will indeed masturbate. When I was young we used to say that 90 percent of the guys masturbated and the other 10 percent were liars.

Masturbation, of course, is self-stimulation, "playing with yourself," as the kids would say. I think another negative association with masturbation comes from the fact that many parents extinguish the natural tendency for youngsters to touch their genitalia with their hands. Many an adult can remember their mom or dad shouting, "Get your hands off your thing!" Of course there are many myths that have always accompanied the subject of masturbation. Myths like, "Your penis will fall off," or, "You'll go blind by Tuesday"; "Your head will be covered with zits within 24 hours"; "Your supply of semen will run out"; "You'll get a bad case of dementia praecox"; "You won't be able to have a baby," are just a few that have been with us for some time.

Can you imagine what the child thinks when, through personal curiosity and experimentation in adolescence, he or she learns that gently touching and caressing the genitalia is especially fulfilling, and that all those myths he's heard about masturbation aren't true? I can almost hear that adolescent saying, "Hey, this isn't so bad."

Masturbation is one way adolescents can safely and, without harm to anyone, relieve their sexual pressures. Now remember that we were created in such a way that we have the capacity for those special feelings. Most adolescents report that their parents did not prepare them for the eventuality of a nocturnal emission—or a wet dream. A young male will have wet dreams in the absence of masturbation during the adolescent years. It's a very natural way for the body to rid itself of the extra semen that accumulates in the young male. Can you imagine the guilties a young male might get if his first nocturnal emission comes and he has not been prepared for its eventuality by either parent? It's important for us to realize that kids are going to have sexual thoughts during adolescence. They might be doing some fantasizing and masturbating; that is all part of growing up.

Although parents in many circles have made masturbation a controversy, I personally don't feel that it's a big deal. It is a normal part of every person's development. I don't see that masturbation causes any harm unless a person becomes overly preoccupied with it. Then it can contribute to an unhealthy thought life and feelings of guilt or lust. To help keep masturbation under control, kids need to avoid sexually stimulating movies, television programs, books, magazines, music, etc. as much as possible. They should also find other outlets—athletics, strenuous work, hobbies for releasing the emotional tension caused by their sexual drives. Masturbation is a personal matter, but it is something each family needs to talk about. Kids have to make a determination concerning masturbation based on their own feelings and experiences.

Dr. James Dobson, in *Preparing for Adolescence,* speaks to the adolescent from a Christian perspective on this delicate subject in an honest, forthright manner:

> The subject of masturbation is a very controversial one. Christian people have different opinions about how God views this act. Unfortunately, I can't speak directly for God on this subject, since His Holy Word, the Bible, is silent at this point. I will tell you what I *believe,* although I certainly do not want to contradict what your parents or your pastor believe. It is my *opinion* that masturbation is not much of an issue with God. It's a normal part of adolescence which involves no one else. It does not cause disease, it does not produce babies and Jesus did not mention it in the Bible. I'm not telling you to masturbate, and I hope you won't feel the need for it. But if you do, it is my opinion that you should not struggle with guilt over it.[3]

Adolescents Long for Freedom

Someone asked me not too long ago, "How do you really know when your child begins adolescence?" Of course I think many people equate the beginning of adolescence with the beginning of the maturation process, that is, the time when our children begin to develop into young men and women. I responded that perhaps even a better way to tell whether or not your child is entering adolescence is to be very sensitive to the first time your 11- or 12-year-old sinks into the car seat as you drive past some kids on the corner. Many parents can recall when they began to give their parents vibes that they wished Mom or Dad wasn't around. This is the beginning of the desire to be free from parental restraint.

Ask a child sometime, "What age would you be if you could be any age at all?" How do you suppose most kids would respond? The most typical age children want to be is 16. Why? What's so special about 16? Well, for one thing they can drive. That's a biggy. Driving represents independence. In the teenager's life today the car is certainly close to being number one. That's one reason why, when counseling parents of adolescents, I suggest that in disciplining teenagers, parents zero in on three things: the car, money and privileges. Those are three things that the American teenager relates to almost without exception.

Adolescence is a time for that longing to be free. It's that very uncomfortable, uncertain time in a person's life when he is neither fish nor fowl. He is hovering somewhere between the innocence of childhood and the awesome responsibility of facing the reality of adult life.

Arthur Fonzerelli, better known as the "Fonz," portrayed by Henry Winkler on the popular TV show of recent years, "Happy Days," is still a popular person with the peer group. Why? The Fonz was cool. And more importantly, the Fonz didn't have any parents. You never saw Mr. and Mrs. Fonzerelli on a program. The Fonz didn't report to anybody. He was free. The free spirit Fonz represented on "Happy Days" is what many teenagers long for. But they aren't free. They have moms and dads who tell them what to do and what not to do; they have younger brothers and sisters who drive them up the wall; teachers who just don't understand and are boring and give terrible assignments; girlfriends and boyfriends who, from one day to another, can't make up their minds whether they like them or not. So, although the longing to be free is great with teenagers, they aren't very free. They are restricted. This lack of freedom is one reason why some teenagers rebel.

Kelly, age 15, is such a case. She came to me at the suggestion of her parents who were concerned about the changes they were seeing in Kelly's life. Kelly's mom was a home-ec teacher, a perfectionistic, a rather high-strung woman, and very overprotective of Kelly. As president of the PTA she had very definite ideas about child rearing, and very definite ideas about Kelly, the youngest of her three children.

Kelly's dad was an easygoing, laid-back professional person, a dentist with a very heavy work load. He was very good at keeping his emotions to himself. Kelly's dad had enjoyed the serenity of their home with the two older sons, now 22 and 18. The older brother was in law school and the other was a freshman at the university.

Kelly was very perceptive and sensitive as to how she should act to please her mother. In fact, Kelly told me she thought her whole life was mapped out for her by her mother, that her mom knew exactly what she should be when she got older, what to study, who to date, as well as what dress looked best on her.

Kelly's parents' concern for her was justified. "We're worried about Kelly," her mother told me. "She's bright, outgoing, an excellent student. But she is also lazy, self-centered and manipulative. She has recently begun cutting classes at school."

At age 14 Kelly showed an inordinate desire to be

with young men. She started dating older guys. This, of course, met with much resistance from Mom and Dad. But, like many parents faced with a kid's constant pleas, they finally gave in.

Kelly began a downward slide very quickly as her fifteenth birthday approached. She became rebellious to the point of being openly defiant to her parents. Out of the blue she displayed a smart mouth as well as language that wasn't fit for the saltiest of sailors. Mom (remember she's the PTA president) started to get a series of calls from school. Not only was Kelly's ditching increasing, but she would show up at school drunk (when she bothered to come in at all) at her 8:30 morning class! Mom and Dad sought professional help for Kelly when school officials caught her in the back seat of a car making out with a 19-year-old student.

As I met with Kelly in therapy it became very clear that there was no way Mom was going to control her life. Kelly was going to show her folks that she was no longer the little girl they wanted her to be. She described her parents as terribly overprotective, archaic, old-fashioned, unrealistic, and boring. She said she was the only one of her friends who had a midnight curfew on weekends. Kelly's whole life-style seemed to say that she counted in life only when she controlled, when she won, and when she bossed her parents around.

I must confess there were times when I felt helpless due to Kelly's great desire to be the opposite of what her mom wanted her to be. Her mom was not very good at following my advice to back off and give Kelly some room, so Kelly had decided she was going to show her. And show her she did! But at what expense! Kelly began a pattern of staying out past her curfew. The more she rebelled the more Mom and Dad tried to clamp down. Finally, one night, she just didn't come home at all.

At age 15 she left home for a period of about 13 months. Of course she was forced to quit school. During this period of time she lost almost all contact with her school friends and found a new group to associate with, some crusty-looking fellows who didn't work regularly and rode motorcycles for enjoyment.

During these 13 months away Kelly was transformed from a relatively naive and sweet young lady into a hard and abused young woman. She went, in short order, from drinking a few beers a day to smoking so much pot that—in her own words—she was so wasted she could hardly see straight.

She finally moved in with three young men, ages 19-22, and shared a one-bedroom apartment with them. During this period of time she had many sexual experiences, not only with the three men she lived with, but with several others as well. She was used in the truest sense of the word. During that 13-month period she got pregnant on two occasions, had two abortions, and the last guy she "went with" left town as soon as he heard he was going to be a father. He was a coke-head and had already fathered two children by age 21.

After 13 months of freedom, Kelly began to make some overtures about coming home. She called me at my office one day and caught me by surprise. I was with a client but took the time to speak with her when I learned it was Kelly on the phone.

"Can I see you?" she asked. We set up an appointment for that afternoon.

When Kelly walked into the office I couldn't quite believe my eyes. Where had the blonde-haired, blue-eyed, pretty little 15-year-old gone? What I saw before me was frightening. She looked rough, beaten-down, and her language was atrocious. She obviously had very little self-respect at that point in her life. I asked her quite directly if she had had it with her new freedom, and was she ready to go home? As she sat in my office sobbing, she nodded her head; she thought it was time to go home.

I called Kelly's parents and they came to the office. The four of us spent the afternoon talking about many of the same issues we had talked about a year earlier: responsibilities, curfews, language, smoking, drinking, pot-smoking, and her general demeanor. We began to make an agreement that both parties could live by.

It was a great personal joy for me to see Kelly want to go home and live with her parents. After all, they were the two people who loved her most in all this world. As I saw them leave the office that afternoon, arm-in-arm, I knew it wasn't going to be easy. It was going to be very difficult to put things together and to heal a relationship that had been so broken.

Since that day more than five years ago I have spent several hours with Kelly, talking about how special she is and about her need to treat herself as special if she is ever going to be in a position to attract people who are good for her, people who have good self-concepts, who would be less likely to create situations where Kelly would continually be used and abused.

Kelly is now living a fairly normal life. She went back to school and essentially allowed her parents to parent her. She didn't always like it. Even today there are still some hassles to be solved, but basically the relationship is healing.

Soon after Kelly returned home I asked her, "If you could tell teenagers one thing, what would it be? What would be your personal advice to others your own age and in the same situation of rebellion?"

She offered two things: "First, try to realize that even though your parents seem out of it they really do love you and care about what happens to you; second, stick it out at home no matter how bad it is. Living out there in the world by yourself is the pits."

Perhaps you're thinking that Kelly is an extreme case; let me assure you she isn't. I have case histories, many of which are very similar to Kelly's, with many of the same hurts, trials, tribulations, and with basically the same results. Given time, teenagers learn that there isn't a better place on earth than home.

Kelly was one angry and resentful young lady who wanted her freedom from a mom who had to make all her decisions for her. Fortunately, for all of them, Kelly came home and they had a second chance. Kelly had learned that she needed her parents. And Kelly's mom had learned to love her daughter with open arms. She had learned to walk the tightrope between giving Kelly the love and guidance she needed, and giving her enough freedom to grow.

Chapter 2

It Takes Guts to Be Different

To what extent will young people go to be accepted by the group?

I believe that one of the most frightening things for us as parents is the realization of what awesome power the peer group has over our own children. Adolescents try desperately to imitate their peers, to accept the mores and the standards of the masses. In fact, recently I worked with a young man who had done a 180-degree turn-around in school—he'd gone from an A student to a failing student. When we got down to where the rubber meets the road we found out that this abrupt change in behavior occurred because of the tremendous amount of pressure he felt from his peers to get poor grades in school. He was an outcast because he had chosen to do well in school and gain good grades.

In his book *Preparing for Adolescence*, Dr. James

Dobson talks about a very famous experiment in social psychology. Psychologists wanted to study the effect of peer pressure on teenage subjects.

In the well-conceived and well-designed study, 10 teenagers were told that they were going to view cards with straight lines on them. They were going to vote by way of raised hands for the longest line. However, nine of the teenagers were told to vote for the second longest line, not the longest line, contrary to the instructions given. The tenth teenager was not let in on these instructions, so there was really only one guinea pig—the one who wasn't told to vote for the second longest line.

Can you imagine the look on the guinea pig's face when nine hands went up in the air, voting for the second longest line? Even though it was obvious that the line was not the longest, out of fear that he'd be different, the guinea pig slowly, hesitantly raised his hand; but he did raise his hand and agree with the group. He didn't have the power of his convictions, even though he knew he was right, to say that the group was wrong.[1]

Now you might be thinking, "Yes, but that's an isolated case. Most people wouldn't do that." Not according to this study. More than 75 percent of the guinea pigs responded in the very same way. This classical social study gives us parents insight into the profound effect group pressure has upon our adolescents.

Do you remember the time in elementary school when you knew the right answer to a question the teacher asked but didn't put your hand up? Why? Out of fear that maybe there was a chance in a million that you might be wrong and you'd look ridiculous to your peers. The fear of rejection is so great in some of us that we won't even try, even when we know the right answer.

Okay. So what does this say to us as parents? How can we help our children stand up for their beliefs?

Encourage Nurturing a Best Friend

I believe that one of the things we as parents can do is to really reinforce and encourage that one special friendship our son or daughter might have. An adolescent's best friends are probably going to be of the same sex. With a little help from you in nurturing that relationship, your teenager will discover a special bond between himself and a friend, someone who will support him when he is faced with a decision that might go against the peer group standards.

With the hectic pace of today's activities it is easy for couples to suddenly discover that they have been parents for 15 years and literally haven't done a great deal with their children. Once the parents get their careers developed to a point where they can spend some time with their adolescents, the adolescents are beginning to be at a point where they no longer enjoy doing things with just Mommy and Daddy; the peer group has taken over.

It may not be too late. Encourage your son or daughter to take a friend along on a family weekend. This will go a long way in strengthening the relationship between the adolescent and his friends. At the same time it will give the family the experience of doing some things together.

Be More Obvious in Your Influence

How many hours a day do you spend with your children? Two? One? Sometimes only a few minutes a day?

In this hectic world it's easy for parents and kids to be isolated from one another. And when we might have time on weekends to spend with our kids our activity-conscious society fills our schedules to such an extent that no time is provided for the family.

We talk a great deal about the "quality" time we give our kids as opposed to quantity time; but, really, all your kids understand is "time." They just need to be with you, to observe your life day in and day out. Of course this puts a great burden on parents to monitor their own lives.

I believe it's a wise parent who tells his kids what he believes and why he believes it. But, above all, it's wiser to *show* what he believes by his life. It does very little good for a parent to lecture on the evils of smoking or drinking while he himself freely indulges in those things.

When I think of the influence we have on our kids' lives I think of a woman I'll call Sally. Sally had a 17-year-old named Sarah. Sarah was a very popular girl in her school. She was a pom-pom girl and an attendant in the queen's court at her school's homecoming celebration. Due to her God-given beauty, inside as well as outside, Sarah never lacked for dates. And to top that off she was a fine student.

One day Sally, Sarah's mother, answered the door. Sarah's 17-year-old boyfriend was standing there. He asked if he could come in. Of course Sarah's mom said, "Sure, come on in and have a seat."

Well, Bob, Sarah's boyfriend, started off the conversation by saying, "Mrs. J., what is it with Sarah? How come I'm not getting any?"

Now I can tell you right now that if anyone ever has the audacity to say something like that to me about one of my daughters he won't live long enough to hear the answer! Sally, however, handled the situation much better than I would have. To say she was shocked would be an understatement, but she managed to pull herself together, look Bob in the eye and say, "You and I have to talk." (As hard as this might seem to believe, this conversation actually took place.)

Sarah's mom went right after Bob. She started out, "When I was 17 I hated sauerkraut, despised it. I couldn't stand the smell of it. It made me want to vomit just to think about it. Today I'm 41 years old and I love sauerkraut. There's not a thing I love more in the world than sauerkraut.

"Now as you know, my daughter and I have a good relationship. We talk about a lot of things. In fact, I know that my daughter is thinking about breaking up with you tonight. The reason is that she is sick and tired of your constant harassing her for sex. I think, Bob, that what my daughter's trying to tell you is that she's not ready for sex. And we hope that when the day comes when she is ready, she will be married.

"I know that's how she feels right now. She's telling you plainly and clearly that she doesn't like sauerkraut and she wants no part of sauerkraut in her life now. And because of your immature attitude toward her feelings she's ready to quit seeing you."

Now if you don't think those words took Bob back a few paces, you're wrong.

Sarah did not stop seeing Bob right away. On another occasion, as conversation developed along the same topic, Bob told Sarah's mom that he felt all kinds of pressure from the other guys in his peer group. Every time, after a date with Sarah, when he saw the group the following morning at school, they asked 20 questions as to how far he got. "Did you get to first base? Second base? Third base? Hit a home run?" The interesting thing is that with the insight given by this wise mom, Bob was able to back off, in spite of peer pressure. When Bob got it straight in his head that Sarah didn't want any part of pre-marital sex, their relationship turned around 180 degrees. Bob was able to resist the pressure from his peer group; he took the pressure off Sarah and the two became *more intimate*, if you will, in the truest sense of the word. They could enjoy each other's company and have fun together. They truly liked each other, especially when the hassles and strains were removed from their relationship.

Think how good the relationship had to be between mother and daughter. If I had the authority or the oppor-tunity to give a mother-of-the-year award, it would go to this mom, this mom who resisted the temptation to tear out that young man's spleen and, instead, sat down to give him some good, wise counsel when he really needed it.

How great it would be if every parent could really talk about everything with his or her adolescent. We as par-ents get very few shots at them as they're growing up. They grow too quickly. We don't seem to have enough time along the way to express to them what's really important in our lives. But when we dig down deep and share out of our own personal lives with our children, that's when we really give carte blanche for them to dis-cuss with us anything they want to. Such a relationship doesn't come naturally. It takes work, hard work, a lot of listening, and a great deal of understanding and a lot of mutual respect and love between parent and child to get to that point.

Your teenager needs your positive influence in his life.

Select the Environment

How much time do your children spend in school? A good guess might be between six and seven hours each day. Here's an area where parents really need to put some thought: Where do you want your children to go to school?

It's no secret that private and parochial school enrollments are surging. Why? Well, there are obviously many reasons, but one answer for sure is that many parents believe the public school system does a beautiful job of teaching irresponsibility; that there is little discipline, closeness or warmth between teacher and child; and too many things are going on in the public schools that are negative influences on our kids.

However, if you decide to send your child to a private school you had better make the decision while he is in the first grade. If you start talking about sending your child to a private school as late as fourth grade, he's going to say, "No, I don't want to go. I don't want to leave my friends." Even by the fourth grade friendships are already established and the peer group is in full swing. I believe that if you want your child to attend a private school you have to make that decision as early in the child's education as possible to maximize the influence of the school's environment.

If you do still have children who are young enough to be placed in a private school, the choice sounds easy at this point, doesn't it? All you have to do is pick the closest private school for your children, or go the public school route. Well, it's not that easy. Suppose you choose to send your child to a private school. You better take a long, hard look at the great variety of private schools available in your community. If your community is like most (larger communities), there are great differences in private schools. If you are interested enough to consider a private education for your children, I hope that you are interested enough to get yourself down to the school while school is in session, with your son or daughter in tow, to observe and get a feel for how things are going to be at the particular school you are considering.

If our adolescents are going to deal with a world that says, "Conform, be like everybody else," then our teenagers must see positive relationships in their family and in their school life—relationships that seem to say that someone really does care about them.

Again, if you have young children, investigate the school where you are considering sending your child. Make sure that it really provides everything your child needs. Because he's going to spend more of his waking hours in schools being influenced by his teachers and his peers than he is going to spend around you. If you choose not to send him to a private school, for whatever reason, then make sure his nonschool hours are spent in the presence of those people and influences you want to affect his life; if you don't make your influence obvious in the very early years, someone else will.

Help Them Adjust to Change

Change affects everyone, but change seems to be particularly stressful to adolescents. Parents have to help their teenagers cope with change; yet, many times the parents are also trying to adjust to the same changes.

Richard came to me a few years ago because he was in great difficulty—he was in trouble with the law. He had just taken part in an armed robbery and admitted to recently participating in 16 home burglaries.

Richard was 17 and the oldest child in his family. His mom, at the time Richard came for therapy, was seeking dissolution of her marriage of 22 years. Now I'm not about to say that if Richard's parents weren't going through a divorce but, rather, had a good, sound marriage, Richard wouldn't have gotten into trouble. I'm not *going* to say it, but I'm tempted to—tempted because it came out in therapy with Richard. The most powerful feelings he had inside of him were the feelings concerning his mom and dad's impending divorce.

I really believe Richard felt that life was being unfair to him, and that, basically, life had kicked him square in the teeth. Therefore, in a democratic society, if life had the right to kick him in the teeth, then he was going to strike back.

Not only was Richard going through a change because of his parents' divorce, but the family had just moved from the Boston area to the Southwest. Breaking into a new peer group is a very difficult assignment for some kids, and it was with Richard. He had to become acquainted with what his peers in this new setting expected of him. He had to reestablish himself in a whole new environment. Although he was an athlete, his sport wasn't played until spring, so he couldn't use baseball as a way of initiating friendships. So Richard felt very isolated and lonely. These two changes in his life really laid the foundation for peer pressure. The need to conform made Richard, who was a pretty good kid, become involved in some things that were very uncharacteristic of his prior life.

One of the other guys who was involved in the armed

robbery had, by chance, been sitting next to Richard in a class and had introduced himself. Richard's first thought was, "At last! A friend!" It may not have been the friend Richard would have picked if he had been able to sit back and pick his friends, but it was somebody—somebody to be close to.

So here's this kid, a pretty good kid who had never been in any difficulty in his life, and suddenly—because he is so desperate for acceptance—Richard finds himself going along with his new friend when the friend pressures Richard into driving the getaway car for an armed robbery, as well as being party to 16 home burglaries. The last contact I had with Richard, he was still in jail.

Adolescents need help in coping with change.

Help Them Say No

It's hard to say no. It takes a lot of character and a lot of self-esteem to do what we know we should.

When I was a little kid, my friend Moonhead and I would walk along the village roads in the summertime, anxiously watching for a driver to flip a cigarette butt out of a window of a passing car. We'd run to get the cigarette butt that we didn't even need matches for. I'm sure we smoked for lots of reasons—to seem like big boys, to impress our peers, to feel more grown up, older than we were. The first time I ever smoked a cigarette I was seven years old, and I continued smoking until I got smart and quit at approximately 22. (Which was also about the same time I met my wife—in the men's room of a local hospital. But that's a long story we don't have time to get into—yet.)

As a teenager I really didn't know how harmful cigarettes could be. There was some talk about how destructive smoking was; today it's even spelled out on the package: "Warning: The Surgeon General has determined that cigarette smoking is harmful to your health." Yet even though it's right on the carton millions of people still smoke. So, although we know things aren't good for us, we continue to do some of those things. It's hard to say no.

Even when we become adults it's hard to do what we should. For example, which day of the week do you suppose is the most popular to start a diet? Mondays, right? Why Mondays? Because Monday, being the first day of the working week, makes it easy on Saturday night to lie to ourselves as we reach for that second piece of pie and say, "Monday I'm going on a diet." Even though we know that all that sugar isn't good for us, even though we know we shouldn't smoke cigarettes, we as adults have a terrible time saying no. Imagine, then, the difficulty adolescents have, with peer pressure as strong as it is, saying no to one hit on a marijuana cigarette or a snort of cocaine (coke). It's extremely difficult. My experience with teenagers is that they consciously know that many of the things they do are really not good for them, but they don't have the self-esteem or the self-control to reject them.

Parents must help their children develop self-discipline, which leads to a good self-image. When we feel good about ourselves, when we can accept the real us, just as we are, then growing up becomes much easier. If we can't have a good self-image then we are headed for a great deal of trouble. We will never really feel that we are worthwhile, that we belong.

There are some grim statistics that highlight the overpowering need for adolescents to belong. If an adolescent doesn't feel that he belongs and has his place, or if he feels rejected by society, that adolescent might end up a tragic statistic. Today, in our country, 13 teenagers will kill themselves. The suicide rate among 15—24-year-olds has risen by almost 300 percent in the last 20 years.[2]

According to the Suicide Prevention Service in Ventura, California, 500,000 American teenagers will attempt suicide this year. Five thousand—or one percent—will succeed.[3] I believe that many of the teenagers who kill themselves do so because they feel that they really can't measure up in this world. The sad thing is, by my observation, many teenagers who have taken their lives were actually extremely good students in school and were very highly thought of by others.

However, the important thing, remember, is how they saw themselves. Maybe they felt that they were unworthy or unimportant. They may have grown up in an environment where Dad pushed the level of expectation so high that the teenager was defeated by the overly-high demands placed upon him. Or, to get Mom and Dad off the hook, perhaps the child placed these high expectations on himself. I haven't seen any suicide statistics among firstborn children or only children, but I wouldn't be surprised to find that there was an extremely high incidence of suicide among these children because of their perfectionistic nature. (See my book, *The Birth Order Book,* for more information on the subject of firstborn children.)

In an article on adolescent suicide, McHenry, Tishler and Christman studied the behavior of adolescents who attempted suicide. The majority of these evidenced the following changes: (1) drastic changes in personal appearance from good to bad; (2) somatic complaints (stomachache, backache, headache, diarrhea, etc.); (3) inability to concentrate; (4) dramatic shifts in the quality of their school work; (5) changes in daily behavioral patterns which could manifest themselves in extreme fatigue, excessive sleeping, withdrawal, decreased appetite, emotional outbursts, use of alcohol and drugs, loss of friends, and an overwhelming sense of guilt and shame.

The investigators also cited crises which are accompanied by the aforementioned behavioral changes: the death of a family member, relative or close friend; separation of parents, siblings or relatives; personal problems with the law or someone close having problems with the law; plus others.

The writers suggest that discussing suicide will not make the depressed adolescent more inclined to commit suicide; rather, he is emotionally relieved by the opportunity to discuss his feelings.[4]

I know it is downright scary even to think about teenage suicide. I really believe we could prevent such tragedies in our teens' lives if we would dedicate ourselves to honest communication with them. That is, when we get brave enough to share some of *our* thoughts and feelings with our children, it gives *them* permission to discuss theirs with us.

Remember, prior to the teen years, plant the seed in your adolescent's mind that the coming years may be stormy ones. Then, when the time comes that your teenager begins to experience some weird, crazy, upsetting feelings, and finds himself tempted to withdraw and keep everything inside, that seed you planted years earlier will germinate and grow and, hopefully, give him strength to ward off some of those feelings of desolation and loneliness he may be experiencing. Then the door will once again be open for you and your teenager to discuss the problems and emotions he is facing. And if he doesn't have to face them alone, he has a much better chance of surviving his teen years intact.

Chapter 3

Dating, Mating and Waiting

Many times I've been asked at my seminars throughout the country, "Okay, Leman, when are you going to let *your* daughters date?"

I reply very matter-of-factly, "When they're 31. And of course on a double date with me and their mother in the back seat."

Since time began, girls and boys have been drawn together like bees to honey. However, in many traditional cultures dating was never an option because the parents of the children chose their future mates. But in our society dating is a very appropriate way to get to know which qualities you are looking for in a lifetime mate.

Now I believe that teenagers should be intimate in their dating—but not physically intimate. As a young man begins to date one young lady more than any others his goal should be to discover as many things about her, and she about him, as they each can. How does she think about certain things? Can he share some of his own burdens and hurts with her? Can he take off his mask and let her see the real him without getting that feeling of rejection?

Why should kids date, anyway? Is it really important? I think it's important. But there are several factors that have to be considered.

Pushed into Dating

From what I have discovered in working with families, many kids start dating because their parents push them into it, sometimes at a very early age.

Have you ever heard an adult say to a seven-year-old child—maybe even to your child—"Do you have a girlfriend (boyfriend) yet?"

Now what does this convey to the youngster? "Gee, it sounds like I'm supposed to get a girlfriend already."

From my observation, children in some circles are being forced to grow up too early. Too much too quickly seems to be in vogue in modern-day America. Parents and peers literally force the young boy or girl to concentrate on "boyfriend" or "girlfriend" rather than just "friends." Kids need to spend several years developing friends of both sexes.

Teens or even preteens often begin dating because of peer pressure. What kids their own age feel and think during the turbulent years of adolescence usually outweighs what Mom and Dad think. So even if you never encouraged dating as your kids were growing up, by the time they are in junior high school dating is becoming very critical to them because of peer pressure.

A Need to Be Noticed

This age has a need for status, a need to be seen with the right person. There is very little emotional feeling for the date, just a desire to be seen with someone. This is very closely linked to the teenager's self-image. The someone he dates—or would like to—has to look "good"—a neat hairstyle, good physical appearance, and "cool." But, unless he meets those standards himself, he won't find anyone to date him. And this is where many young people meet head-on with an identity crisis. They really want someone to notice them.

Everybody, at any age, wants to be noticed. Nobody wants to be neutral, invisible, a nonperson. But this desire to want people to notice us is particularly strong during the adolescent years.

When I was a college sophomore I got myself in hot water with school officials. One evening the ice cream machine in the dorm where I lived went on the blink and began to give away freebees. All us students went down and proceeded to rip off the machine. Of course the dorm lost a lot of money in the course of the evening. The head resident put up a sign near the switchboard to the effect that, "All of you who participated in the unauthorized ice cream social the other evening, please put your money in this box because the dorm lost x amount of dollars."

My roommate and I came in, saw the sign and the money, and also saw the old gentleman who sat at the switchboard, sound asleep. We looked at each other with the same thought, *Wouldn't it be funny if we ripped off the conscience fund?*

Well, we ripped it off all right, and like most 19-year-old kids who do something to be noticed, we had to tell the whole world. So we threw a party for the guys in our wing. It didn't take long for word to get down to the head resident and on to the dean of students that Leman and his roommate were responsible for ripping off the conscience fund.

We had wanted to be noticed—we were! We were kicked out of school—a lot more notice than we'd bargained for.

Teenagers have a need to be noticed. They will go to great lengths to be noticed by the peer group, especially the opposite sex. They reason, "How will I get dates if nobody sees me?"

Necessity—The Mother of Invention

I had always been rather curious about the dating habits of college students, so while I was at the University of Arizona campus I did a survey to determine just how many students dated at least once a week in the dorm system. I discovered that a surprisingly low 15 percent of the college students dated on a regular basis. One might think that on a college campus of 35,000 students there would be all kinds of opportunities to date. Although daily they walk by literally thousands of members of the opposite sex, these students have very little opportunity to really be noticed or get to meet someone.

Now I personally think that by the time an adolescent reaches college age he should be dating, so I encouraged the students I worked with to meet people. I'll never forget one experience I had. Four young coeds who had heard me speak at freshman orientation took me up on my invitation to come visit me in my office if I could be of service to them. They were all a little apprehensive because they didn't know what to expect. But one young woman who seemed to be the spokesperson for the group popped off about not being able to meet any men on our campus.

Well, I explained to them that there was a big difference between high school and college and now they would have to take things into their own hands and sort of create the kind of environment that would attract the type of boys they were looking for. I asked them if they would be willing to do something a little crazy. They looked at each other inquisitively and gave a halfhearted shrug of their shoulders, which I took to mean that they were willing. I suggested that they take a popcorn popper to one of our largest men's residence halls, go into the lobby, sit down, and begin popping corn.

You can imagine their feelings, thoughts and expressions as they walked into Santa Cruz Hall on the University of Arizona campus, complete with popcorn popper, oil, butter, popcorn, some bowls and a sheet to spread out on the floor. They told me they kept looking at each other as if to say, "I can't believe we're actually doing this. I feel so stupid." But they spread out the sheet, plugged in the popcorn popper and began to pop corn. As the popcorn aroma worked itself up the stairwell of the men's residence hall, about 40 guys, like bears awakening from a long winter's nap, lumbered toward the lobby area. Forty to four—those aren't bad odds for anybody!

As it turned out the girls had a great time. And did they meet guys! Some of the guys thought it was a pretty good idea too because, as the evening wore on, four of them stayed around and paired up with these four young coeds and they ended up going out for pizza after the popcorn bash. The following evening these four guys retaliated with a popcorn party in the girls' dorm.

So when dating begins to get critical your teenagers may have to take matters into their own hands and create situations where they can meet others. But they must be sure the situation is going to draw the kind of guys or girls they want to meet. Remind them about the singles who go to the singles bars to meet Mr. or Miss Right only to find they've met someone who wants to do nothing but hang around bars.

Being Noticed for the Right Reasons

I can think of one young lady I recently worked with who tried to get men to notice her by hitchhiking. She got three men to notice her real well. They picked her up, took her off in the desert, beat her, robbed her of her money, forced her to perform several sex acts with them, and then dumped her in the desert, naked.

Teenagers want to be noticed. They want to think that they are special, above the norm. Yet by their very nature they see themselves as very awkward, gawky, uncoordinated, and klutzy. Although many teenagers see themselves that way, parents must see each of their children as very special, and treat them that way. They should spend time with them and show that they think their kids are special. It's in these early experiences that self-concept takes root.

It's important for a child to learn that he is good and capable and that Mom and Dad, brothers and sisters care for him. If we are able to create an environment within the home where a kid can grow and learn about himself and others without a constant fear of rejection or ridicule, then that growth can be positive.

So many times I see parents become tremendous flaw-pickers, pointing out all the shortcomings and faults of their teenagers. This kind of discouraging experience during those turbulent adolescent years can do nothing but drive the kid from home and get him hooked into whatever's in vogue in the peer group.

People often ask me, as I'm speaking across the country, why so many of my examples come from very young children. I do that because the training up of a child really occurs in the first seven years of his life. If we don't catch them then, chances are we never will. After all, teenagers can really do whatever they want to do in life. It's only out of respect and love that they allow their parents to parent them at all. The teenager who really wants to be rebellious and give his parents the hassle of their lifetime can certainly do so.

Setting the Guidelines

Okay, I know you're reading this book and you have a 16- or 17-year-old son or daughter and you're thinking, "Thanks a lot, Leman. What am I supposed to do—go back in a time machine?"

Of course not, but one of the things you could do at this stage if you haven't been a responsible parent, haven't disciplined your kids, haven't tried to put things in proper perspective, is to start with an apology to your son or daughter, and then say, "Things are going to be different from now on." The plus of that is you can always make a shot at turning things around.

Now, let's get down to talking about dating regulations. What about dating? What's this whole area really all about? What is accomplished by dating? What are some of the guidelines for dating? When should a teenager begin to date?

Of course, each individual kid is different, but I think 16 is a good age for a kid to begin dating one-on-one. I think in group dating situations kids can certainly be dating as early as 14 or 15, as long as they understand that dating is permissible at that early age only in groups.

There's a tremendous danger in letting teenagers begin dating too early. I had a 15-year-old girl tell me once that she was absolutely bored with dating. She started so young that she kept progressing further and further in order to keep the dating experience exciting. Now she was so sick of getting drunk, stoned, smashed and making out that she'd had it. She wanted time out from guys. She felt that she had been raked over the coals too many times during her first 15 years.

Dating, regardless of all the social problems of the peer group, should be a time of having fun, sharing time with somebody else and getting to know each other. But your teenager is going to need some help in setting guidelines. I believe the teenager in your home who is about to start dating should be encouraged to prepare his or her own guidelines for dating. Most kids basically know the problems that exist with dating, and most of them really don't want to get themselves in a situation they can't handle.

For instance, I know of a 16-year-old girl whose parents allowed her to set her own curfew at midnight. Let me tell you, those parents were pleasantly surprised to find their daughter coming home from her dates at ten or eleven. This is not at all unusual when teenagers are trusted to set some of their own guidelines. So let them prepare a list of do's and don'ts. I think that's a far healthier way to start than for Mom and Dad to issue an edict on how things are going to be. One thing we know about young people is that if they have any input into rules and regulations there's a higher probability that they will adhere to them. Of course, there will have to be some discussion between parents and kids concerning the list, and probably some give and take as well.

Getting Physical

Too many young people try to make dating a purely sexual time together. They do this for many reasons, but the primary reason, I think, is, again, peer pressure. They are coerced into proving themselves. The sexual drive is there, but they must be taught that, like everything else in life, it should be put under control. The choice is rather clear: either we control our emotions or our emotions control us.

The tragedy of it all is that if young men really knew how young women felt about sex they'd be shocked. You see, the most special physical act according to women is not sex, but just being held. Let's face it, there's going to be some kind of physical touching between a young guy and girl as they go through the dating process. They're going to be holding hands, kissing, touching in some way, shape or form. Many of them are going to move on from there to petting, and, as statistics tragically demonstrate, many of them will become involved in intercourse as well. But just as men don't understand women, and vice versa, so boys and girls don't understand each other's distinct needs and specialness either.

An article I read years ago really demonstrates for me the difference between young men and young women.

The study was reported in *Psychology Today*. Researchers found, in a study of 432 young people, that teenage boys and girls looked at things quite differently from one another. Teenage girls who wore hip-hugging jeans and no bra tops thought they were just being stylish. To the boys who looked at them their fashion suggested that the girls wanted to have sex.

Other conclusions of the study by four members of the Department of Psychology at UCLA found that both sexes agree that if a girl accepts a date with a guy who has a fast reputation she should expect the boy to come on strong during their date. Interestingly enough, relative to my earlier comment about girls just liking to be physically held, the girls were more likely to agree with the statement, "Sometimes I wish girls could just be friends with boys without worrying about sexual relationships."

Someone along the line really sold us a bill of goods about men and women being the same. Men and women will never be the same. We were created distinctly different, which doesn't mean that we have less than equal social value. But the point is that men and women are different.

The Courage to Be Different

Dating for young teenagers today is difficult, to say the least, in a world that really attacks the very center and sanctity of the special way in which we look at sex.

The dating experience can be a rocky one. There are lots of hills and valleys. There are going to be many tears and heartaches, ups and downs. But if teenagers are able to develop friendships with other kids who believe as they do, if they realize that they are special, and if they don't want to get themselves into situations where they're used or are using someone else, then I believe, with God's help and sheer determination on their part, teenagers can get through those tough times with minimal scrapes and scars.

As I told a couple of parents just a few months ago, our goal with teenagers is to be able to get them through the teenage years without them killing themselves or without someone else killing them. It's difficult to be different, especially when the whole peer group says everybody's got to be the same. But if your son or daughter really wants somebody special in life, if they really look forward to marriage as being something unique where two really do come together and become an entity within themselves, a loving relationship that is nurtured with mutual respect and love, then they're going to have to have the courage to be different, to speak their mind, to learn to say no, and to be very selective about whom they date and with whom they associate.

Hazards of Premarital Sex

We've already said a bit about premarital sex; as a marriage and family counselor, I feel I must say more. There's a great deal of pressure on teenagers to engage in premarital sex. This comes not only from the peer group but from society in general. Kids are forced to grow up too soon, and to complicate matters, every place they look they are bombarded by the media with all different forms of sexuality. Advertisers have learned that sex sells.

The Bible has a great deal to say about sex. However, let's forget for a minute the many scriptural admonitions against fornication and adultery, and concentrate instead on the hazards posed by premarital sex.

I'm sure you've heard a lot of statistics about the problems young people encounter because they engage in intercourse before they're married, but let me refresh your memory.

Children Having Children

Sexually active young people can now get advice on birth control methods without ever letting their parents know about it. But as the experts tell us, many young people don't use birth control, even when it's available.

There are probably several reasons for this. The first reason is very difficult for adults to understand: many a young woman who feels alienated and unloved by the significant others in her life—her mom and dad and her family—might really want to get pregnant. The fantasy of having her own little baby sounds wonderfully attractive to a young teenager who feels that life has dealt her an unfair hand of one kind or another.

Such teenage naiveté is exceeded only by stupidity. It's only after that young adolescent has given birth to a child that she begins to realize the awesome responsibilities she has incurred by choosing to get pregnant. So even though it's a common assumption about how young men are always looking for young women to score on, let it be known that there are many young women who are looking for just the right young man to father their first child.

Another reason why many girls might not use birth control methods is that they were brought up with traditional Judeo-Christian values. In this case, using birth control would indicate they are planning to sin or to go against God's laws, thus it would be a very guilt-producing experience for them. I recall one young woman of 16 years of age who was sexually active with her boyfriend of 18. Although the young man wanted to practice contraception by use of a condom, she wouldn't let him. She said she felt it would violate her religious practices. (Psychologically, as long as she could avoid facing the reality that she was actually choosing to be sexually active and accepting the responsibility for that choice, she could claim innocence by saying, "It just happened.")

I suppose the most obvious reason teenagers don't practice birth control is that many of them simply don't live a very structured or planned life. In the process of not taking the time to think about what their physical and sexual limits are in the dating relationship, many teenagers find themselves in situations where one thing just leads to another. In the height of passion it's very difficult and cumbersome to take time out to use contraceptives of any kind. There is a tendency in some teenagers to be so caught up in the fantasy of lovemaking that they don't want any interruptions, even that of protecting themselves from pregnancy. Did you ever see a movie where, during one of those titillating love scenes, the young lovers stopped to use a contraceptive? It just doesn't seem like the romantic thing to do.

Venereal Diseases Becoming Deadly

We need to reinforce another very ancient danger connected with premarital sex—venereal disease. (Of course venereal disease is not confined to premarital intercourse, but many states require blood tests from couples getting a marriage license so that they can become aware of any venereal disease either of them may have before they marry.)

In an article entitled "Did He Leave You with More Than a Memory?" (written in 1980) the author says that there are more than 20 sexually-transmitted diseases. Of these, five must be reported to the Department of Health by your doctor because they are so hazardous to health and are highly contagious. The five are: syphilis, gonorrhea, chancroid, granuloma inquinale, lymphogranuloma.[1]

Three lesser-known sexually transmitted diseases, which, as of 1980, did not have to be reported to the Department of Health, are now occurring in epidemic proportions: nongonococcal urethritis, genital herpes, and trichomoniasis.[2]

The American Social Health Association estimated in a 1980 report that from five to twenty million Americans have herpes. The number is growing at the rate of approximately 500,000 cases a year.[3]

Since that article in 1980, an even bigger menace has hit the venereal disease scene—AIDS (acquired immunodeficiency syndrome).

AIDS cripples the body's disease-fighting immune system, and leaves its victims vulnerable to a variety of life-threatening infections and even certain cancers.

AIDS is primarily transmitted through sexual contact, although it can also be transmitted by contaminated blood transfusions or the sharing of contaminated hypodermic needles. AIDS can also be passed from a mother to a child at or before birth.

According to the Centers for Disease Control in Atlanta, as of September 22, 1986, AIDS has been diagnosed in 25,515 people in the United States and has claimed 14,097 lives.[4]

Although AIDS in the past has primarily been confined to male homosexuals, the disease has now "crossed over" and is infecting heterosexuals as well. One of the main reasons that AIDS (as well as other venereal diseases) is spreading so quickly is that every time you go to bed with someone, you are actually going to bed with that person's other sexual partners too. Since the incubation period for AIDS can be up to five years, a seemingly healthy sex partner may already be infected.

At this time, there is no known cure for AIDS. And, unlike some of the other venereal diseases, once you have contracted it, you must learn to live with it if there is no cure. AIDS is a disease you die with. That's scary.

Looking for Love in All the Wrong Places

With the exception of AIDS, veneral disease seems to be the hardest on girls and women. This favoritism doesn't stop there. There's always pregnancy.

An Associated Press article about unwed mothers said that "nearly one in three white teenagers and more than four out of five black teenagers giving birth in 1979 were not married" (Census Bureau statistics).

According to an article by Scott Kraft in the *Santa Barbara News Press,* "This is all happening despite the fact that birth control is more widely available and abortion is more accepted. Among the reasons, experts say, is that more women want to marry at a later age and there is less of a social stigma for an unmarried mother who decides to keep her child."[5]

Although the above reasons appear to be valid, I

think the problem still goes back to a situation that exists today in most homes in our country, and that is that many of our teenagers feel alienated and unloved by their families. Going through the turbulent adolescent years with little perceived love or security in their lives, many teenaged girls essentially *choose* to get pregnant. That is, they feel they need to love something, and more importantly they need something to love them.

The sad truth is that few teenagers are mature enough to take on the great responsibility of raising a child. These teenage girls who feel that they have this great amount of love to share with another human being would be wise to adopt a kitten from a local humane society. All parties concerned would be much better off.

The cycle perpetuates itself in a home where the pregnant teenager chooses to keep her own baby. The greatest thing a father and mother can do for a child is to love that child with all their hearts. That's obviously very difficult when there isn't a father in the home.

So the cycle gets repeated once again: the young teenaged daughter, with the encouragement of others, keeps her child, then pawns the child off on Grandma—literally. Over a period of years Grandma develops a maternal relationship with the child, rather than a grand-mother role. I've seen young mothers go off to college and chase down bachelor's degrees as well as master's degrees while Grandma is raising the child.

It's a wise teenager who has the foresight and courage to give up her child for adoption to a young couple who can't have children of their own. The question has to be asked, Whose needs are being met by keeping the child? Does the mother have her own best interests at heart, or her baby's? Tough decision for a young kid to make.

Ignoring the Statistics

People Magazine, reporting on information from the Alan Guttmacher Institute, says that almost 90 percent of teenage mothers are deciding to keep their babies, and nearly one-half of the nation's illegitimate births are to teenagers. They go on to say that between 1970 and 1978 the number of sexually-active teenagers increased by 50 percent. By the age of 19 only one-fifth of boys and one-third of girls have *not* had intercourse.[6]

Thirty thousand girls, aged 13 to 14 years old, conceive each year.[7] These young mothers under 15 are five times more likely to die during childbirth than women aged 20 to 24. And infant deaths are twice as high among babies born to teenage mothers.[8]

According to an article entitled "Adolescence and Sexual Behavior" by Dr. Kevin O'Reilly and Dr. Sergi Aral, printed in the *Journal of Adolescent Care, 1985,* "teenagers now account for almost one-third of all the abortions performed in the United States each year."[9]

Many of us tend to ignore statistics such as these, until we become one of them. These statistics come from some of the periodicals young people read—*Mademoiselle, Ms., Senior Scholastic,* etc. And high school and college students are taught these facts in their various classes. But they don't hear them until their parents take an interest in their welfare and point out these very prevalent problems to them.

Taking the Responsibility

Are you brave enough to take the responsibility to open up and talk to your teenager? Let's face it. It's difficult to talk to anyone about sex—even more difficult to talk about sex with your son or daughter. Again, because no one ever talked to us, right? It would be so much easier if we could just slip a brochure under our teenager's door filled with all the facts that we would like them to know. Then just attach a note to the brochure, "If you have any questions at all, please feel free to contact me at my toll-free number at my office." But you see, teenagers need more than just information. What teenagers need is love and understanding, and a commitment on their parents' part to get involved in their lives.

I can't think of a better way to become involved with your teenagers than to share some real life experiences that may not only show your teenagers that you are not really the product of the Dark Ages, but that you do realize the many struggles and temptations they face. When you're brave enough to share some experiences from your own life, then your teenager *might* be willing to share some real thoughts and feelings with you too.

Now's the Time

If you're wondering about how to get started on something like this, if you haven't had a regular time of getting away with your son or daughter, you might be wise to start right now. Now you're probably thinking, "Wonderful. Sure. My teenager is just going to love to go away with Mom or Dad." But remember, you have to learn to walk before you run. I suggest that you begin to make some inroads in this area. Touch base with your teenager by taking him or her out for lunch or dinner. Let your teenager choose the restaurant. Then after you have made a few attempts—feeble as they might be—to establish intimacy with your son or daughter, plan a family weekend away together, or perhaps a weekend with one of your children and yourself.

I know it's difficult to find time for these things, but as most of us parents are aware, our kids grow up too quickly. I know my own schedule is a tremendously hectic one, yet I've taken my children, one at a time, out of school on business trips with me when I'm conducting a seminar or doing a television program in another city. It's a very unique time that we have together. We have fun and we laugh, but more importantly we have some time just for the two of us, and my children look forward to this very special time. They would literally forsake any of their own activities to hop on an airplane and go with me. We always come back closer and with a better understanding of each other, and we both feel like it was well worth it.

If the thought of a heavy conversation with your son or daughter is scary even to think about, start with something light. Have you ever told them some of the crazy, foolish, dumb, weird things you did as a teenager? Kids thoroughly enjoy listening to Mom's and Dad's antics as teenagers. What a great way to show your children— who think you were actually classmates with Tom Edison and Benjamin Franklin—that you truly were a kid at one time.

Think just for a moment about where you got all of your information about sex. Didn't you get it from other misinformed friends? Or from dirty stories or restroom walls? Research tells us that very few people are privileged enough to get a good, honest, open dialogue going with their parents. This is a crime for us parents. To not talk about one of God's greatest gifts is a tragedy that is relived in many lives today.

Living Together

Before we stop talking about "Mating" I feel it's important to cover another subject that is becoming more and more of a problem—living together. It used to be called "shacking up," but we've come to accept it as a normal thing so we've dressed up the description.

Kay and John were a typical example of couples I see in my private practice so often today. John is 23, Kay is 22. They lived together for two years and have been married for only about six months. The day after they got married things began to disintegrate. All of a sudden they were confronted with problems that never existed when they were living together. They were legitimately confused and puzzled when they came for marital therapy. I say they're typical because John and Kay and thousands of other couples like them made a judgment error. They really thought that living together was a foolproof way to test whether or not they were compatible for marriage.

You really can't blame them for thinking along those lines. It does seem to make sense, on the surface, that living together might be a good way to really find out if it would work for them. The Census Bureau reports that the number of couples living together has more than doubled since 1970. Nancy Evans, in *Glamour* Magazine, lists several reasons people give for living together.

1. One out of three marriages end in divorce, so why bother? (The statistics are now closer to one out of two.)

2. It would be a lie to promise to love somebody forever. People change in the course of their lives, and not necessarily the same way.

3. Why ruin a good thing? Marriage somehow changes relationships for the worse.

4. Marriage is constricting. They don't want to make a commitment. This last reason emphasizes "me" rather than "we" which results in greater expectations from marriages than it did in past generations.[10]

Why is it that so many couples really get along fairly well while they live together but when they get married things don't go half as well? I think the key is commitment—or lack of commitment. Living together is the heaviest form of dating. It isn't the same as a marriage commitment because couples who just live together never entirely take off their masks. They are still on their best behavior, as they are on their dates. They don't become the true people they really are.

Living together is a commitment not to make a commitment. The couple who lives together has an open-ended agreement with each other. In a marriage, however, the commitment is to each other and is made in front of everyone (including God), and the consequences of breaking that commitment seem greater. Of course, stakes are much higher in marriage than they are in living together. You really have more to live up to when you become a husband and wife.

We live in an age when commitment is looked down upon in many quarters. However, when it comes to that true intimacy that so many young men and women apparently yearn for, it can only be attained through marriage. Furthermore, recent research tells us that the success of a marriage is probably not enhanced one bit by living together before marriage.

Living together is certainly not the way to fly, even for practical reasons—such as very little financial protection, no security, no retirement benefits, and a few other legal protections in general. Especially for a woman, there is very little security in a live-in relationship.

Some Basic Differences

In addition to the aforementioned practical reasons, perhaps more important to a woman are the emotional scars that remain throughout her lifetime. On the basis of my working with hundreds of couples during the past decade I have come to the conclusion that there are several basic differences in men and women. One of the most obvious to me is the fact that as men we are able to separate the physical and emotional quite easily. I've had men tell me that they've been good husbands and have had only five, six or eight women during their marriage. For whatever reason, men seem to be able to distinguish between physical relationship and emotional relationship more easily than women. The fact remains that women, more so than men, tend to carry the emotional scars of a relationship that doesn't last.

For many women, guilt associated with living together prior to marriage is an added burden that they must carry through life. Even though they intellectualize their living together, and on the surface appear to have rejected their parents' values as well as the religious instruction they may have received as a child, for some reason they are unable to shake these guilt feelings. Even if they later marry the man with whom they have lived, many of them suffer a great deal of guilt. The guilt is really a two-edged sword that has to be dealt with, whether the guilt is precipitated by violating their own personal standards and values, or whether they violated their parents' values and standards. It really is a rare individual who can reject family values and live a life-style contrary to those values without suffering from a certain amount of guilt.

Learning Some Lessons

A couple of times in this book I'm going to share with you a transcript of a tape from one of my clients. Chuck, who came to me in his early 20s seeking direction for his life, gave me permission to pass this on because he hopes someone will be helped by his experiences.

"Premarital sex is something I would never have dreamed I'd be talking to anyone about because, along with alcohol and dope, as I was going through school, sex was also the thing to do. You weren't cool if you hadn't been laid in a while. I remember how embarrassed I'd be when I told my friends I hadn't been laid by a certain girl I went out with. It just wasn't cool. It wasn't really until I'd grown up a little bit that I found out just what kind of adverse effect premarital sex has. Especially for the woman. I hate to say that; I hate to sound biased, but especially for the woman.

"I have a good friend who shared how she and her boyfriend were madly in love. They just knew they were the right ones for each other. They engaged in premarital sex—she gave herself to him literally, because in sex the two really do become one. Premarital sex puts a strain on a relationship because the relationship then becomes just physical. Instead of meeting and talking, sharing your day, going to a movie, just enjoying being with each other, you get together, have sex and leave. Just to fulfill your needs, you might say.

"Anyhow, this friend and her boyfriend, after a couple of months, found out that they weren't right for each other, they weren't meant to get married. She's 21 years old, a college graduate and a beautiful girl. As she told me about this I could see in her eyes the hurt she had gone through. She said she would wake up in the morning and vomit blood because she was so upset. She had given herself to somebody and he wasn't the right person, and she couldn't get back what she had lost. It's kind of like giving someone a million dollars and later finding out you gave it to the wrong person, but now he's gone and so is your money. Gone for good. You don't have it anymore. And the person who should have had it will now never get it.

"I recently started going out with a girl that I knew a few years ago. One thing I admired back then, really liked and respected about her, was that she wasn't messing around with anybody. Even when I was messing around with drugs and alcohol I still had a high ideal of what I wanted in a girl, and this girl was my kind of woman because she didn't give in to guys. Well, after I became a Christian and changed my life-style, this girl came back into my life. We started going out to dinner and talking and sharing our lives. It was just beautiful. She was just as lovely as she was the day I first met her.

"One day she shared some experiences she was struggling with. She said that she had made love with this guy. She looked at me and said, 'Chuck, if there is some way I could just turn back the hands of time . . . ' I don't think this guy was worried about it, but I can guarantee you she was. He had given her the ultimatum that 'if you love me you will,' and she did, so she did. She never felt right about it and it really had a traumatic psychological effect on her.

"Then when we were having dinner one night she told me about another guy. She thought she was going to marry him and lived with him for two years while she went through college. I can't tell you what her telling me that did to me. It was like a slap in the face. Here was this girl I thought was so special, that I had such high regard for, telling me that she lived with somebody for two years. For some reason that just didn't set with me right. I had hoped that the woman I would fall in love with and marry would share all the little deep secrets of her mind, her feelings and her philosophy with just me. I think when you're lying in bed with different people all of the time it's kind of hard to know who's special and who's not. Don't get me wrong. She wasn't laying around with a lot of different people, but living two years with a guy, a lot of things can happen between them.

"But when I talked with Dr. Leman about this he explained to me that I had taken away a lot of those special things from girls I had sex with in high school. That really hit me. Some of those girls know in the back of their minds that they will have to share our experiences with the ones they fall in love with. I can imagine how those boyfriends are going to feel. I feel it once, but I might have caused it 10 times.

"I know one girl who told me she doesn't hold or kiss or anything on a date. By today's standards that's kind of hard to believe. She's a beautiful college girl; but she doesn't want to get trapped in any kind of a relationship until she gets married. She wants to keep all her dates on a friendship basis. I think that's neat."

It's Hard to Wait

As we said before, it seems that teenagers want everything life has to offer them—and they want it all at once.

It's hard to wait. But when teenagers rush into a sexual relationship or marriage or independence, almost without exception it ends up disastrously.

Many young people have, of course, a great amount of ambition and determination. When your daughter finds the right man, even though he may have a few faults, she figures, "Oh, he's going to be different after we're married. He says he'll start going to church (quit drinking, stop running around, get a job)." She is naive enough to think she can change the other person.

If I just love him enough he'll change is a fallacy to begin with. There's no way that any of us can change another person, not someone we're married to, or a son or daughter or mother or father. All we can do is change our own behavior, which might, in the long run—and sometimes that's a real long run—help the other person change his or her behavior. If a teenager is really set on marrying a person who has all the qualities he or she is looking for, then it wouldn't make sense to date any other kind of person, would it?

Trapped

Cheryl was one of those women who was determined that things would work out. She and Dave were in love. After seven years of marriage, steadily growing farther and farther apart in their relationship Cheryl did something that she ended up regretting deeply—she had an affair with a young married man.

The affair lasted about a year and a half before she came to grips with the fact that her lover was never going to leave his wife. Cheryl was really trapped. She was trapped in a marriage where she had grown more and more distant from her husband, and now she had gotten herself into an affair that was literally tearing her up.

Any situation that would create dissidence between a couple and divide them should be avoided. Marrying someone who doesn't believe as you do is asking for trouble. Today Cheryl is still trying to put the pieces of her marriage back together, but she isn't getting much cooperation from Dave. And even though she's absolutely guilt ridden by her affair with the married man, she is still very much in love with him; however, he has shown very little interest in wanting to see her again.

Unrealistic Expectations

The thing we need to express to our teenagers is that if they have an idea of the kind of person they want to spend their lives with, then they'd better look for those qualities in future marriage partners now. After they're married there is very little chance of changing anyone. In fact, they might discover that the things they disliked about their future mates only intensified after marriage.

Do you suppose that when a young couple walks down the flower-strewn aisle of the church on their wedding day that they're thinking about getting a divorce in a few years? No, I don't think so, either. But statistics show that the average marriage today lasts just seven years. That's one of the reasons why it's so fundamentally important for us to understand the very temporary nature of early romantic love. Many couples run blindly into relationships that are primarily physical. Physical intimacy in a sense takes the place of a sincere relationship so that young lovers are robbed of the opportunity to really get to know each other. They don't get a chance to talk, communicate or even think, much less share experiences. So they end up getting a very unrealistic view of love and marriage.

Short-Lived Relationships

Kathy and Ron were married at age 16. Kathy was escaping from an unhealthy situation in her home—her father was abusive to her and she very much needed the comfort and "love" of a male. Ron also had an unhappy home life. His mother was an alcoholic, so he too wanted to run away from something.

So these two people, who had great amounts of insecurity, were literally forced together in love. Unfortunately, the love was not a lasting love but a physical love, a love that went by the wayside very soon after they were married. Kathy had two children by Ron and, by the time she was 19, was divorced with two young children.

These young people made a mistake in judgment that could have been avoided. Kathy and Ron both had poor self-concepts. Because they were insecure they sought out people who would give them comfort and fill that void in their lives. Unfortunately for that insecure young couple, when things got rough after they were married and they really needed to communicate with each other and rely on something other than their physical relationship, they had nothing. Absolutely nothing. There was no choice but to go their separate ways.

Learning from Mistakes

We all make judgment errors and do foolish things. Hopefully, we can learn from our mistakes. We as parents need to try to impart this to our children. The only way we can do this effectively is to tell them about some of our own mistakes. Sometimes it's very difficult to expose our weaknesses to them. But when we do, it gives them strength and encouragement to be open and honest with us.

I think of my own two daughters who one night were with me at a softball game. I'm a fast-pitch pitcher in a city recreation league. It was the first inning and I wasn't even in the ball game. I was simply coaching first base because the other pitcher was on the mound that evening. Well, in the first inning the umpire made an unbelievably poor call on a high pitch and I yelled out, "You're crazy."

The umpire jumped out from behind the plate, took off his mask and shouted down the first base line, "What did you say?"

And I said, "You're crazy."

He said, "You're out of the ball game."

And I retorted, "Well, I'm out of the ball game, but you're still crazy."

The rules call for players to leave not only the field but the entire park when they're thrown out of the ball game. Well, needless to say, I was embarrassed. It was honestly the first time I had ever been thrown out of a ball game of any kind and I wasn't even playing. My two young daughters were with me and they were just getting a good start playing on the swings and slides and rings in the park when I called to them, "Come on girls, we've got to go home."

They looked at me rather astonished and said, "Home! We just got here. Why are we going home?"

I said, "Come on, get ready to go home. Get in the car. Hurry!"

They reluctantly went along and began to press me for a reason when we got to the car.

Well, I found myself about to lie to my children, tell them some kind of fish story, but I caught myself. I turned to my younger daughter Krissy and said, "Krissy, what happens when you talk back to Daddy?"

She looked at me, puzzled, and answered, "We get sent to our room?"

And I said, "Yeah, that's right. Daddy just talked back to the umpire, and the umpire sent Daddy to his room."

My children understood that one perfectly. So perfectly that the first thing they blurted out as we entered our home several minutes later was, "Mommy, Mommy, guess what? Daddy got kicked out of the ball game."

So the lesson is, when *we* make mistakes, our kids can learn from them.

Chapter 4

Getting, Scoring and Conquering

One night, not long after my second book, *Sex Begins in the Kitchen*, was published, I was tucking my nine-year-old daughter, Holly, into bed. As we had on previous occasions, we spent some time talking about sex. I think Holly had a pretty good notion of what sex was all about, but I really wanted to talk with her rather matter-of-factly about the nitty-gritty of intercourse. I explained the physical act of intercourse as simply and directly as I could. No sooner had I gotten the words out of my mouth than Holly looked up at me and exclaimed, "How gross!"

Well, I must admit, I laughed out loud. But how else would a nine-year-old girl think about intercourse? Although nine-year-olds aren't generally overtly interested in the opposite sex, my experience has shown that nine-, ten- and eleven-year-old children spend a great deal of time thinking about the opposite sex, and about sex as well. It's a shock to many of us as parents, who are used to having our little girls and boys climb up on our laps, to discover that suddenly they are becoming all grown up.

Do you remember the first time you accidentally walked in on your 11- or 12-year old while he or she was getting dressed? If your experience was anything like what happened to me when I blundered in on my daughters, the chewing out you got probably rivaled that of an army private at boot camp. Children are rarely subtle when they let us parents know that things are changing in their lives and that they're quickly hurtling themselves toward the world of adolescence.

Let's Talk About Sex

It might be hard for some of us parents to realize that our teenagers will, by the time their seventeenth birthdays roll around, have ample opportunities to have sex. And the statistics of teenagers' sexual activity are disturbing, to say the least: 80 percent of boys and 67 percent of girls under 19 have experienced intercourse.[1]

Of the approximately 21,000,000 adolescents in the U.S. between the ages of 15 and 19, 11,000,000 are estimated to have had sexual intercourse at least once. And of the 8,000,000 13- to 14-year-olds, 1.5 million are estimated to have had intercourse at least once. Approximately 30,000 girls ages 13 to 14 conceive each year.[2]

Now these statistics are enough to scare many of us parents into some kind of action. But what is disturbing about this whole thing is the fact that teenagers are ignorant of the realities of sex. Authorities—counselors, physicians, pastors—point out repeatedly that teenagers have many misconceptions about sex: sex at mid-cycle is safe; conception can't occur the first time they have sex; coitus interruptus is safe; etc.

When you think of sex, what do you think of? Something nobody should talk about? Something shady or forbidden? Or do you think about something that's really neat, wonderful, priceless, and truly a gift? I hope you think about it as a gift, because that's what it is. It's really a gift from God. In fact, sex was God's idea first. And He planned it; it wasn't simply an afterthought He had. God created us as sexual beings.

Think about the time you, as a husband or wife, had perhaps the greatest sexual experience of your married life. You ought to be smiling now. Are you? Where did that ability to reach that pulsating orgasm come from? Where did those special feelings come from?

We have the capacity to be sexual in the truest sense of the word, even at birth. Studies indicate, for example, that male infants still in their mother's womb have erections. Kids at a very early age discover the pleasure of self-stimulation of the genital area. We are made in such a way that we can experience these feelings right from the very beginning. These are natural feelings, not dirty, nasty or "down there." Then how did most of us adults, and adolescents as well, get such a negative perception of sex?

One reason is that parents aren't able to talk with their children about sex. We find it very, very uncomfortable. And, of course, we parents are uncomfortable because our parents never talked to us about sex.

As a psychologist it's necessary for me to talk to people about their sex lives. I do that routinely with almost everyone I see. When I first began private counseling and had to ask the question, "How's your sex life?" I'm here to tell you that it made me very uncomfortable. It was something, like everything else, that I had to learn to do.

Our kids usually hear very little from us parents about one of the most important forces in our lives—our sexuality. We neglect to counsel, warn and advise them about the use or misuse of this important part of our lives. As a matter of fact, most teenage girls find out whether or not they are pregnant without any assistance from their parents. Parents need to keep communication lines open with their teenagers on the subject of sex, as well as other areas.

There's Only One Right Way

Darrell Royal, former University of Texas head football coach, once said that there were three things that could happen when you made a forward pass, and two of them were bad. So it is with sex.

Sex is for married couples, between husband and wife only. These seem like hard words, especially in light of today's values. Yet there are many reasons, besides the biblical ones, why teenagers should avoid becoming sexual athletes. But every Monday morning, in every locker room on every high school or college campus, you hear guys asking each other, "Did you score Friday night? What did you get?" And you know what they're talking about. There seems to be some kind of a contest to see who can conquer the most girls the fastest.

It's hard to figure out why two 15-year-old girls would have a race to see who could lose her virginity first. This was the case of one of my young clients and her girlfriend. It's hard to believe that they would want to have sex that first time when research strongly suggests that a woman's first sexual experience is not a satisfying one.

Katherine Bement Davis told of one study with 1,000 educated married women. The study found that one-fourth of them were repelled by their first sexual experience.[3]

There seems to be similar agreement along that line in many other studies. Paul Popenoe, director of American Institute of Family Relations, found that in a survey of 658 women only 25 percent of them achieved a normal climax at first intercourse. Only seven percent achieved climax in the first 30 days, an additional 26 percent between one and eleven months, 16 percent one year or more. Six percent reported never being able to attain a normal orgasm.[4]

My 15-year-old client reported to me that her first sexual experience "hurt like hell." Her date was very drunk, left her in the park, and drove himself home. In many circles of young people today it really is a cool thing to lose your virginity, the earlier the better. This young girl won the race all right, but what a price she had to pay.

One of my observations about people is this: they want what they can't have. A teenage girl who refuses to let her body be used, who doesn't follow the crowd in the sexual contests but seems to be a little different from everyone else, is a cut above all the rest. She truly is someone who is worth dating, pursuing, admiring and caring for.

Sex is a gift, and teenagers can accept that gift. That's the easy part. The hard part is to make wise decisions concerning its use. The key is to keep themselves out of situations where they are used or abused in any way, shape or form. People are for loving; things are for using.

It is important to teach our teenagers not to use others, and not to let others use them.

There will always be somebody who will gladly use others for his own satisfaction. Whether that person is a young man or a young woman, there are plenty of them around. The thing is that we have the freedom to decide how we're going to conduct ourselves. But as the Fram Oil Filter man tells us, we can pay now or pay later. We can follow the rules and enjoy life to the maximum or abuse them and pay for it the rest of our lives. It's our decision.

So, what are some of the reasons why teenagers should decide not to have sex before they are married?

It's All Right to Say, "I Don't Want To"

Many teenagers know they aren't ready for sex yet. "I don't want to" is a pretty good reason not to have sex. It's the only reason anyone really needs. If a person finds himself doing things in life that he really doesn't want to do, sooner or later he's going to become very confused, angry and resentful. We need to reaffirm our right to say no. (Many of us had our early inclinations to say no beaten out of us by parents who insisted that children didn't have the right to say no.)

Traditionally, many a girl has told herself, "I gave myself to him. He said if I loved him I would prove it to him." In the 1980s women can no longer blame men. All of us are responsible for our own actions. Young women who allow other people to control their emotions by telling them what to do with their bodies end up being very unhappy women someday with husbands who tell them what to do and how to do it.

One thing is clear: each of us is responsible for our own actions, and each of us needs to work on being in control of our emotions rather than having our emotions control us. But, you ask, aren't young men and women going to get together in some way, shape or form? Of course they are. Like moths to a flame, young men and young women will find each other. Where we fail as parents is that we issue an ultimatum to our teenagers to not do anything. Now that's unrealistic. When young men and young women get together there's going to be some kind of physical activity. But it's the wise teenager who knows that he or she must set limits. Again, we keep coming back to: Yes, but where do we draw the line? Hold hands? Kiss a little bit? Make out a lot? Pet just a little bit? Or heavy petting? Just how far does one go?

First of all, I think it's unrealistic to think that a teenager should have the same limits for all situations. For example, there might be a young man that a young woman is not especially interested in; she may not even want to hold his hand or show any kind of encouragement to him on her first date. By mentally setting an all-inclusive limit she is creating a bad situation. Nobody should feel like she has to hold hands with someone she's not interested in.

Teenagers have a tremendously high need to be wanted, but most of them do not really want a heavy sexual relationship. They only submit out of fear of being rejected. But if somebody really cares for you and loves you, they're not going to demand their own way. That is really counter to what love is. So each of us really has the right to say no. And we all—adults and children—need practice in saying no; it's okay to say no. You don't have to do what everybody else wants you to do.

Remember the "sauerkraut example" when the mother explained to her daughter's boyfriend about why he wasn't getting anywhere sexually with her daughter? The daughter was saying no to her boyfriend. She wasn't about to be pushed into something she didn't want to do. Like all other skills it takes practice to say no. The teenager today, facing the turbulent world of adolescence, is going to have plenty of opportunities when he or she should say no. There's a sea full of people out there who are ready, willing and quite able to use others for their own hedonistic satisfaction.

I used to run around with a guy in high school who even went to the extreme of having notches on his belt. Let your mind wander at this point and guess what those notches represented—conquests, scores. What a terrible way to look at something as special as sex.

Pregnancy Is a Pretty Good Reason to Say No

The second reason for saying no to sex is to avoid unwanted pregnancies—either your own or, if you're a boy, your girlfriend's. The statistics are appalling. Every year more than one million teenage girls get pregnant. Thirty thousand of them are under 15 years of age.[5] Nearly one-half of the nation's 543,000 illegitimate births are to teenagers. If the present trend continues, four out of every ten young women will have at least one pregnancy while still in her teens.[6]

The threat of pregnancy is an excellent reason to say no, isn't it? Most of our teenagers are at the highest level of sexual drive that they'll have in their lives. This fact, accompanied by the ignorance most adolescents have about sex, contraception and the basic facts of life, creates a tremendously explosive and tragic situation. Even if pregnancy is tragically terminated by abortion, many times the experience is the final chapter in a relationship between a young man and a young woman.

As human beings we have a way of telling ourselves that things that are unhappy or unpleasant won't happen to us. I recently had the misfortune of having my wallet stolen from my hotel room when I was on the road. The funny thing was that I remember wondering about the wisdom of leaving the wallet in the room. I even checked the lock on the door to see if it was a substantial lock, and then made a conscious decision to leave the wallet there. "It's just once, and nothing will happen," I told myself. Well, it happened. A thief came into my room, used both of my credit cards, and put $3,300 worth of charges on one card and $3,500 on the other.

Many a teenager plays Russian roulette with sex. I don't know if it's a subconscious way of dealing with their basic desires to bear a child or if it's just a lie that they tell themselves to allow them to enjoy something that basically isn't very good for them. But, simple as it sounds, ask any teenager who has turned up pregnant and most likely she will tell you that she really never thought that it could happen to her. She may have thought that she was too young to conceive. Or perhaps she held the misconception that, on first sex, she couldn't conceive. Infatuated teenagers are somehow oblivious to the realities of life.

Remember that special day when your first child was born? Perhaps the new mother was lucky enough to have her husband with her. What a special day to see that little life come into the world. I know when my firstborn came into our lives I marveled at the majesty of it all. I remember looking through the glass of the nursery and thinking that she was the most beautiful baby in the entire nursery. And as I watched her, tears filled my eyes and streamed down my face—tears of joy and admiration, an overwhelming feeling of how special that little life truly is.

I think in contrast to Amy, age 16, who after four counseling sessions broke the news to me that she was pregnant. I think she needed some time to check me out and see if I was worthy of sharing this secret she had shared with no one else. A child giving birth to a child— Amy was going to do it all without letting her parents in on it. She had things all worked out. She and her boyfriend were going to be married. It was really special because Gary loved her and she loved Gary. I had the feeling that Amy didn't really believe what she was saying, but she did a pretty good job of trying to convince herself as she tried to convince me.

It was no surprise to me, and perhaps no surprise to Amy, that Gary suddenly got interested in a private school on the east coast and disappeared from the community without even saying good-bye to her. He literally left her holding the bag. Did that deter Amy? Not one bit. Amy decided that she would keep the baby. She and the baby were going to have a great life together. Research tells us that Amy is very much in line with what other teenage mothers do. Almost 90 percent of teenage mothers today are deciding to keep their babies.[7]

Life isn't easy for Amy these days. I ran into her a couple of years later in a restaurant where she was bussing tables. She worked the lunch and dinner hours and then hustled off to her one night school course. She told me that it was very difficult for her to get to class on time because many times she had to stay over and work late. In our short conversation I learned that Amy's 54-year-old mom was caring for Amy's child. I was left with the impression that the child was really more the grandmother's than Amy's.

My concern is not only for Amy, but for her little daughter. I'm wondering, without a father in the home, how Amy's daughter is going to learn about men. And I'm wondering if there's ever going to be a time in Amy's life when she finds a special man to love her and her little daughter. I certainly hope so, but realistically, even at the tender age of 18, Amy has two strikes against her, and so does her daughter.

The possibility of an unwanted pregnancy is a very good reason for saying no to sex before marriage.

Trapped in an Unwanted Marriage

A third reason for saying no is that an unwanted marriage might be thwarted. I've personally met older couples who have been married many years, but never really loved each other and were actually trapped because they felt they had to get married because she was pregnant. Some couples, even when pregnancy isn't a factor, deceive themselves into thinking that they love each other, or more often, are driven to marriage by guilt feelings because of their sexual experience with each other. I know that might seem crazy in this day and age, but as we continually see, guilt takes its toll on people of all ages. It's the smart ones who avoid situations in their lives where the guilties are going to do a number on them.

In this day of contraceptives and abortion you'd think such a thing would be rare. I've never taken a survey of the number of my clients who have had abortions, but the percentage is extremely high. However, the anti-abortion group is very large. Many people do not believe in terminating a pregnancy by abortion. So, of course, the alternative is to have the baby. Thousands of families can't handle illegitimate births, so thousands of teenagers face "shotgun weddings."

I recently worked with a 28-year-old woman and her 29-year-old husband, Randy. I started out seeing them together because they were complaining of marital diffi-culties. As our therapy progressed it became evident that Debbie was very depressed. I told Randy I wanted to spend several sessions with Debbie alone.

Debbie and Randy were brought up in rather strict homes. By the time I saw them they had been married about 10 years. They loved each other but things just weren't right. Debbie and Randy had a 10-year-old son, Greg. Greg got along beautifully with his father, but terri-bly with his mother. This was part of the problem with Debbie and Randy's marriage.

After our third session together I asked Debbie what I had a hunch was really the big question. "Debbie, were you pregnant when you married Randy?" I'll never forget Debbie weeping in my office as she shared with me that she had been pregnant and she felt they had to get mar-ried. The pressure she sensed from her own family told her that.

They were married when Debbie was just three months pregnant and she resented that she had to get married. But Debbie and Randy never talked about "having to get married" after they walked down the aisle. She finally divulged her private thoughts to me that, for the past 10 years, she really thought Randy felt trapped and married her only because he had to.

What a joy it was to work with Debbie and Randy and to open up some avenues of communication between them. As it turned out, they loved each other very, very much and they would have married regardless of Greg's impending birth. Debbie's being pregnant at 18 and Randy having to go to work in a bottling company at 19 was no piece of cake. Randy today, at 29, is just finishing his college education. It's been a very tough road for them because of the way their marriage began. Life has a way of holding us accountable for our decisions.

Debbie and Randy had to get married. It so happened that they really loved each other and now, after some counseling, they are on their way to having a happy marriage. But thousands of couples who didn't love each other "had" to get married. Their hopes of finding someone to love were dashed by making a wrong decision, the decision to have sex before marriage.

That Ages-Old Curse Is Still Around

Another reason to say no to sex before you are married is because of the reality and threat of venereal disease. (We discussed venereal diseases in the previous chapter.) Many venereal diseases do not readily respond to medication and can cause a lot of grief before they are brought under control, if, indeed, they can be controlled at all.

Quite some time ago I worked with a couple who was going through the trauma of discovering that each of them suffered from a venereal disease which led to Julie's having her ovaries removed. Julie and Mort had dreamed of having a family. And Mort's mom and dad were very anxious for grandchildren. Mort was the only son of a very traditional Jewish family. He and Julie had to deal with a lot of overwhelming agony and remorse during their time of counseling. I can't remember ever feeling as sympathetic toward a young couple.

Before Julie's operation their life appeared to be so bright, with so many promising things in the future. But the one thing they both wanted the most was now prevented—they were unable to have children of their own. I wonder what Mort and Julie's advice would be toward the young people who, like the majority of teenagers in our country, are considering being sexually active.

What About "Flashbacks"?

Another reason for saying no to sex before marriage is "flashbacks." We live in a time when teenagers are very blasé on the subject of sex. Young men and women go from one casual relationship to another. Having worked on a college campus for several years, I've watched young coeds come on campus and, two weeks into the semester, I've seen them move out of the dorm and in with their special friend of the opposite sex. At the conclusion of the school year they would break up and return home for the summer job. In the fall they would either live together again or find a new partner. The casualness of these relationships is alarming when you see the high stakes our young people are playing with. I'm wondering if the time is going to come in their lives when they wish there weren't six or eight or many more sexual partners in their background.

Ann, age 33, came to me on referral of her gynecologist. She and Michael were married when she was 26. He walked into her life after Ann graduated from college and was just what she always wanted in a man. During their seven-year-marriage she had confused sexual feelings, and was able to reach orgasms only when she fantasized about someone else while having sex with her husband. That was disturbing enough to Ann, but what really got her down were the times she wanted to be close to her husband because he was such a special person. He was a good father to their two children, had a good job, was attentive; he was a good husband all the way around. Because of all these plus qualities in her husband, Ann became more and more distressed with her "flashbacks." She asked her doctor to refer her to a psychiatrist or psychologist. She had to find a way of dealing with the problem.

She told me that when she made love with her husband, as she looked into his eyes and felt his arms around her, the thought of one of her previous lovers would pop into her mind. She said, "As I look into my husband's eyes, I see Jack or Ron or Steve. I didn't even like Steve; it was a terrible relationship. But the thought of these men is affecting my desire for my husband. And now Michael and I are having tremendous sexual problems in our marriage."

Ann's many sexual lovers were taking a terrible toll on her marriage to the only man she really loved. So, although it has become vogue to throw out the old-fashioned tradition of remaining a virgin until marriage, there certainly are many practical reasons for abstaining until then. Flashbacks, although not one of the reasons typically listed for saying no, is one that's worthy of consideration.

Conflicting Values

You might be thinking at this point, "Okay, why should a 17-year-old girl, going with a young man, abstain from sex? They are both virgins, so VD isn't a valid reason. Her boyfriend says he'll take the responsibility of birth control, so pregnancy isn't a concern either. Since they're both virgins, they won't have flashbacks of other lovers if they marry." That brings us to another reason.

It's not only flashbacks that cause guilt feelings. I find in my practice that sometimes—not just months or days after premarital sex—even years later, the guilties are still doing a number on a young man or a young woman. The emotional impact of guilt continues to gnaw incessantly away at a person. Some couples have reported the lack of enjoyment in sex after they marry even though they had a fulfilling sex life prior to marriage. But guilt as a result of premarital sex prevents these couples from experiencing full sexual enjoyment in their marriages.

The guilt feelings come about because they have broken their own moral standards or their family's moral standards. If they have never really grown up and faced family values and made legitimate decisions to reject family values, then these values are still with the child, even if the "child" is a grown adult.

But the question remains, what do you tell teenagers about how to get out of compromising situations? It's great to have six or seven intellectual reasons why one should not engage in premarital sex. But intellectual reasoning might be a little difficult to handle for a 15-, 16- or 17-year-old kid who is just about at the very height of his sexual drive, while he is with his girl in the back seat of an automobile or in a dark room. How can we as parents help our kids in this vital area?

Help Them Set Standards of Their Own

I think we can help them to form standards of their own. Acknowledge that the standards they form might be different from yours; however, they very well may end up the same as yours. It's important to grant teenagers the right and the freedom to make those decisions concerning themselves. Being alone with a girlfriend or boyfriend is obviously a time when they are on their own. They should realize that if they break their own standards, they're going to feel guilty about it. Also acknowledge to them that there are going to be times they wished they could indulge; they're going to be tempted and the temptations are very natural. But the question is, are your teenagers going to allow their emotions to control their behavior, or are they going to consciously control their emotions?

When we don't act responsibly, if we abuse the gift of sex by treating it with a so-what attitude, someone's going to end up paying for it. Unfortunately for women, they seem to get the dirty end of the deal more often than men. Let's face it, women bear the children and are often saddled with the responsibilities of both motherhood and fatherhood while more often than not the man gets off scot-free.

The Courage of Our Convictions

One evening I was addressing a group of athletes on the topic they had asked me to speak on—sex. I told them as best I could from my experience of working with young people that, although it was very difficult, it was best to abstain from sex until they were married. Well, I must admit I felt as if I were talking to a brick wall. I didn't sense much support. I was sinking fast and I was about to run out of words and throw in the towel when I saw a hand go up in the back of the room.

In front of about 60 fellow athletes this young man named Dave got up and said, "You guys know Sherry and me. You know that we've been going together for almost three years. I want to share something with you that Dr. Leman just said that really hit me right between the eyes. Six months ago Sherry and I made a commitment, or recommitment I should say. We were very active sexually. We love each other very much and, as you know, we're planning a summer wedding."

About this time I knew something was coming that was going to be good and powerful; I was all ears, just sitting back like the rest of the guys, listening. You could've heard a pin drop as Dave went on to say that he and Sherry made the decision six months before to quit having sex. He said, "I want to tell you guys that our level of *intimacy* has gone up 100 percent since we stopped having sex."

That young man finished up the evening for me. I didn't have to say another word. I concluded my talk at that moment and went to an informal time of sharing and answering questions. What a joy it was to see that young man get to his feet and say what he did. I'm sure it wasn't easy for him to get up and expose the intimacies of his life with his fiancée in front of 60 athletes, but he did, and that made the difference.

Chapter 5

Love, a Four-Letter Word?

Parents, do you remember when you fell in love? There's not a feeling like it in all the world. Now let's see, the first six times I fell in love, some of the things I remember are the excitement of getting a girlfriend, the thrill of giving her a friendship ring, and the disappointment at learning that she left it in her jeans' pocket and it got totaled in the wringer washing machine.

I guess I did fall in love six or seven times, and each time seemed a little more wonderful than the first. But of course the love I'm talking about is what we commonly refer to as puppy love. Everybody falls in puppy love. Even parents did at one time. So here again is an opportunity to dig into your memory bank and tell your children some of the happy moments you had during your puppy love experiences in your adolescent years.

I think it really helps if we can tell kids, prior to their adolescence, that they are probably going to experience some of the same things we did. Somebody is going to come into their lives who is so special they can't wait till morning to see him or her again at school. Puppy love makes young men all of a sudden become compulsive about brushing their teeth and combing their hair, and sneaking a little bit of Dad's after-shave. Or it makes a young girl stand in front of a mirror trying out special smiles, practicing looking cool and disinterested, or combing her hair into perfection so Mr. Right will think it's naturally that way.

When I Found Love

What is love? How do we know the difference between infatuation and real love? I remember the day I met my wife. Of course, our meeting was more memorable than most because, as I mentioned to you earlier, I met her in the men's room at the Tucson Medical Center in Arizona—well, sort of.

I was a janitor and she was a nurse's aide. I knew there was something special about her from the very beginning. I had seen her on a few occasions around the hospital and a couple of times she had said hello to me; but I could never quite muster up any response other than "good morning." By the time our eyes met that fateful day in the men's room she was probably beginning to wonder if I was, in fact, a little weird. Maybe I'd better explain.

I was a janitor and I was cleaning the men's room. You know how the janitor puts one of those mobile trash barrels in the lavatory doorway to let everyone know he's in there working? Well, I was just emptying some trash into the barrel at the door when my wife-to-be came around the corner. Our eyes met and I blurted out, "Do you want to go to the World's Fair with me?" (Of course, the World's Fair was in Seattle that year.)

She stopped in her tracks and said, "Pardon me?"

That's how we got going. I invited her to go out for a hamburger and I ordered one McDonald's cheeseburger and cut it in half with a plastic fork. My stomach was so nervous I couldn't even finish my half. I shook inside just looking at that woman—she was that special. That was almost 25 years ago and it's really been a very special relationship. The first few days, weeks and even months were a great time of infatuation.

We both laugh at the fact that, on our first date, I couldn't get half a cheeseburger down because my stomach was churning so. If you visited my home and watched me eat now, after being married for about 20 years, we can prove that infatuation doesn't last. That warm, glowing feeling isn't always there. But infatuation can turn into real love as every day, week or month we get to know each other intricately well. Our initial infatuation with each other grew into a steady, loving relationship with which we're both very happy. But that love grew to that point only by the process of sharing and giving, not through taking. I don't really consider myself "lucky" to have such a wonderful wife. Although I love her as friend and mother of our children, I really feel that our relationship is a special gift from God. We have both worked at nurturing and protecting and cultivating that very special gift.

What Is Love?

People have been trying to define love for centuries. A very famous chapter in the Bible, commonly known as the Love Chapter, describes how we can know we're in love. When Paul, the author of 1 Corinthians 13, describes the criteria for true love he starts out with two things that love always *is*—patient and kind. Then he lists several things that love *never is*—jealous, envious, boastful, proud, haughty, selfish, rude. Then he follows through with what love *does not do*—demand its own way, act irritable or touchy, hold grudges or notice others' mistakes. He ends his description with what love *does*—rejoices when truth wins, is loyal no matter what and always believes in, expects the best of, and defends the one who is loved.

Love is patient. One thing that dating does for young people, if they approach dating with the right attitude, is give their relationship a test of time. Time is something many of us, especially young people, have a great deal of difficulty with because we want instant gratification. We live in a time of instant everything—from instant Jello, to soup, to TV dinners. So why not instant intimacy with dating? Why not? Because love is *patient.* Love needs time to get to know the other person. True love can wait until marriage for physical intimacy. Any guy who tells a girl that she can prove her love by having sex with him doesn't know what true love is. Love is patient.

Love is kind. We must be kind enough to recognize that the differences we see in our mates are assets in the relationship and not liabilities. We must focus on the positives in the relationship and minimize the negatives. We need to encourage each other in all things, take the time to say, "Thank you, you were sweet to do this"; "I appreciate your saying that." Through our actions toward our own mate, we need to show our teenagers how to try to think of nice things to do for their girlfriend or boyfriend.

If they begin the habit of being kind before they are married, chances are they will continue to be kind to their mate after they're married. Kindness is essential to a good relationship.

Love is never jealous, envious, boastful, proud, haughty, selfish or rude. Does your teenager feel threatened when someone is around his girlfriend? When a person of the opposite sex talks to your teenager's special friend, does he or she get a little sick feeling in the stomach? That's jealousy. True love trusts the other and is not jealous.

Teenagers need to learn to be truly glad for their boyfriend or girlfriend when he or she accomplishes something or gets some kind of recognition. If she gets better grades or a better-paying job or makes the dean's list, does he feel envious? Or maybe he's the one who gets good grades, has the best job or makes the dean's list. Did he boast about it to his true love? Was he unduly proud or haughty?

Does he listen to his girlfriend, or is his goal in life just to have her listen to him? Communication is really a two-way street, never a one-way filibuster. A person who demands all the attention is usually the one who is boastful or proud.

Do they treat each other with respect? Do they give in to the other's desires and wishes? Do they have a relationship that's built upon respect? Do they ever resort to language that is unbecoming or vulgar? What about name-calling? These actions fall in the categories of selfishness and rudeness.

Parents, are you setting the example for your teenagers in your own marital relationship?

Love does not demand its own way, act irritable or

touchy, hold grudges or pay particular attention to the other's wrongdoing. Love never "gets back" at the other or tries to "get even." Love never demands its own way. I think if I could pick one part of the Love Chapter to measure all relationships with it would be this one: Love does not demand its own way. The other person's feelings are more important. How do you stack up here with your husband or wife? Can your teenagers learn by watching you?

Love is not irritable or touchy. It's the little things about our loved ones that drive us up the wall. Teenagers and their dates often argue over stupid things. Really big arguments can be touched off over little things. Real love overcomes that.

Love doesn't hold grudges or notice the other's mistakes. Puppy love is a bone digger. It's good at looking back into the past and finding a fault and throwing it up to a loved one. It seldom asks for or gives forgiveness. Real love forgives.

Love always rejoices when truth wins, is loyal no matter what and always believes in and expects the best of and defends the one who is loved. A relationship that is not built on truth will never be a lasting relationship. A life built on anything other than total honesty is probably going to have all kinds of difficulties before it. If we really love someone we will be loyal to that one no matter what the cost. We will always believe in him, always expect the best of him, and always stand our ground in defending him.

What does all this mean? It means that love goes on forever, and perhaps the most critical test a relationship will endure is the test of time. I don't know how many times people have come to me for marital therapy and have said, "We fell in love." Yeah, they fell in love all right; and in the process they hit their heads and forgot what love is really like. They don't treat each other like they love each other. They don't do kind things for each other. They don't put the other's feelings first, they put their own feelings first.

The Stages of Love

The authors of several books have talked about the stages of love. They usually list them as: (1) romantic love, (2) friendship love, (3) agape love. A relationship between a man and a woman that is true love really requires all three, not just one or two.

Romantic love is that sensual, sexual kind of love. It is really revelling in the newness of a marital relationship. What a special time this first stage of love is. But if a couple never gets past this first stage, if their relationship is based solely upon the physical relationship, they're in trouble. Because when the tough times come along, their relationship is going to come up short.

Friendship love needs to be developed. Prospective marriage partners should really be very best friends. They should talk to each other about everything. They should enjoy being together. They should ask themselves this question: If I found out that I didn't have much time to live on this earth, if I only had a few days left, would I want to spend those last days with that one I've given myself to?

The third level is the level that couples need to continually strive for—*agape* love. Agape love is sacrificial love. Agape is the love that helps us put the other's feelings first. Agape love is not found on the first date, or the first year, or maybe even the first five years of a relationship. It has to be developed and nurtured.

When most people talk about love they're talking about a tinsel kind of love—a love that's not lasting, based primarily upon the sensual and the physical; that's not real love.

Love and Sex Are Not the Same

In the book *Dating, Waiting and Choosing a Mate*, by H. Norman Wright and Marvin Inmon, is a chart that shows the difference between love and sex. The authors preface the chart by saying, "Often people associate sex with being intimate. But there is a difference. There are different types of intimacy. There is also a difference between sex and love. Some people say that they have loved another person when they have had sex with him. But that isn't necessarily true. Many people have sexual intercourse but love has nothing to do with what went on. Notice the differences between love and sex" (p. 107).

The problem as I see it is that adolescents, particularly girls, need to realize that sexual intimacy is not an indication of love. There will always be people who will use and abuse others. It's hard to fathom a person who would put razor blades in Halloween apples so that little children would be hurt or who would encourage an incestual relationship or who delight in degrading the dignity of human life. But there are all kinds of people in the world, and some of them are out to hurt and harm others.

The solution is to determine who is good and who isn't, or who is good *for you* and who isn't. I worked with a young divorced woman several years ago. She had been through some rough times. Now that she was

LOVE...

... is a process; you must go through it to understand what it is.

... is a learned operation; you must learn what to do through first having been loved and cared for by someone.

... requires constant attention.

... experiences slow growth—takes time to develop and evolve.

... is deepened by creative thinking.

... is many small behavior changes that bring about good feelings.

... is an act of will with or without good feelings— sometimes "Don't feel like it."

... involves respect of the person to develop.

... is lots of warm laughter.

... requires knowing how to thoughtfully interact, to talk, to develop interesting conversations.

... develops in depth to sustain the relationship, involves much effort, where eventually real happiness is to be found.

SEX...

... is static; you have some idea of what it is like prior to going through it.

... is known naturally; you know instinctively what to do.

... takes no effort.

... is very fast—needs no time to develop.

... is controlled mostly by feel—that is, responding to stimuli.

... is one big feeling brought about by one big behavior.

... is an act of will—you feel like it.

... does not require the respect of the person.

... is little or no laughter.

... requires little or no talking.

... promises permanent relationship but never happens, can't sustain relationship, forever is an illusion.[1]

divorced she was seeking a new relationship. I said, "I know it's hard for a 27-year-old woman to meet men."

Connie replied, "Oh, no, it isn't. My roommate meets guys all the time."

I replied, "Oh, gee, that's interesting. Tell me how, because I have a lot of divorced or widowed women coming here who are looking for ways to meet a man."

She answered, "It's really simple. She just goes to a bar and buys herself a drink. Pretty soon some man will buy her another drink, and they just sort of talk."

I pressed the point further to see what transpired. Connie's roommate would end up either at her apartment or his and, of course, have sex.

I looked at Connie and asked, "You mean to tell me that she can meet a guy, let him buy her a cheap drink, maybe even two or three or five, and then within a two-hour period she's in the sack with the guy?" She nodded. I said, "Connie, if that's what you call meeting people, you're kidding yourself. You can always meet people like that. But nothing permanent will ever come out of that kind of relationship."

Filling a Need

There's an amazing similarity between a 27-year-old divorcée and a 16-year-old adolescent girl. They are both vulnerable and very susceptible to being used. And they are both starving for love and affection. This is usually because they had a poor relationship with the father or husband or both, so they go through life looking for some kind of permanent relationship with males, only to come up empty and dry.

Parents, tell your daughters that if their boyfriends

want them to "prove" their love by having sex with them, remember that the boys are not willing to prove their love by waiting until they are married. True love has to be developed. It can't be proven by the sex act. Tell your daughters not to let any guy use or abuse them for whatever reason.

Your daughter can find the kind of love that is lasting, satisfying and meaningful if she demands time to develop it. Not only will she do herself a favor, she will also do her boyfriend a favor by letting him know that she is too special to be used. Guys soon recognize who the special girls are, and they will seek them out as lifetime partners.

Someone once said that women give sex in order to be loved. I think there is a lot of truth to that statement. But a girl should ask herself, "Do I really feel loved when I am in the middle of intercourse? Do I feel cared for after it's finished, or do I feel used?" Almost all women tell me that the times when they feel loved are when they are caressed, treated with respect, and looked upon as special. I think a letter to Ann Landers said it best.

Dear Ann: In a recent column someone wrote about a husband who was unable to perform sexually after a prostate operation. A penile implant was suggested.

My husband has been impotent for three years (also prostate trouble) and he is only 59. We have a wonderful life together—in every way. The sexual aspect of our marriage is much more satisfying to me than it was with my first husband, a handsome and virile man who demanded sex seven nights a week and twice on Sunday. But he knew nothing about making love—for him it was purely a physical exercise, a highly impersonal act. There was never any caressing or words of endearment. He showed no interest in me beyond the fact that I was the vehicle for his bedroom acrobatics. Although he was very bright in other areas (an intellectual), his ignorance and insensitivity never failed to amaze me.

I do not miss sexual intercourse in the least. I am completely satisfied with tender caresses and loving kisses. I adore being held close. Falling asleep in the arms of my beloved is my idea of heaven.

Believe me, Ann, I wouldn't have that stud back for all the money in the world.—Had It Both Ways.

Dear Both Ways: I wish a copy of your letter could be attached to every marriage license issued in the Western world. Since it isn't possible, perhaps it might help to leave this column on the pillow of the man who needs to see it.

How strange that many males who consider themselves enlightened—even sophisticated—don't know the difference between having sex and making love.

When women write to me about this problem I encourage them to communicate their feelings. Some men need to be told what is pleasing. And some women need verbal guidance, too. A mutually satisfying sexual relationship is not a gift—it is an achievement. And well worth the effort.[2]

Sex is a wonderful gift and, when used and developed *correctly,* it can be very beautiful. But it is not the way to build a solid, lasting relationship. The very act of sex, which can bring new life and joy, can also, through misuse, bring destruction and devastation to many lives.

Chapter 6

Twenty Rules for Survival

Adolescents are famous for wanting the best of both worlds. On one hand they say, "Get out of my life, leave me alone, give me space." On the other hand they say, "Hey, Mom and Dad, take care of me. Every time I get in a hassle or need a few extra bucks I want you to bail me out."

Adolescents live on emotions. One day they're sky high and the next they're valley low. Consequently, the emotional life of the teenager is usually topsy-turvy, not by design but by their very nature; and often they end up hurting those who are closest to them—their family members.

What's the best way for us as parents to handle these kids during their teenage years? The easiest way is to say, "If we just love them enough everything will work out okay." This couldn't be further from the truth. Love is not complete without discipline.

Now *discipline* doesn't mean to punish only; discipline means to teach, to disciple, to show the way. Parents need to give guidelines, set limits, establish rules, and enforce them.

Many parents, although they have head knowledge about the rules and regulations that are necessary at home, suffer from the good-parent complex. They have a difficult time trying to enforce the rules and regulations for fear their children might, in fact, reject them.

Guidelines are important because they communicate to our children that we care what happens to them. The kids may not always agree with our guidelines, but that's all right. They also need something to bounce off of, to resist if you will, because resistance is what builds strength. Regulations which teenagers resist will help keep them on a course that is instructive, not destructive, and will help them build the muscle they will need when they are on their own, making their own decisions. So children, for their own sakes, must be taught to respect and obey parental authority.

There is a message that we have to impart to our children: (1) they have to respect and obey us as parents; (2) they are special people, therefore, (3) they have a right to expect the best life has to offer them.

Okay, easy said. Now how do we go about setting up the guidelines that will impart these truths? Following are 20 tried-and-true steps you can take on a day-to-day basis with your children to keep open communication with them until they can stand on their own.

1. Don't Threaten

If you say something is going to happen by way of discipline, be sure it happens. Don't say anything unless you intend to follow through. There's nothing worse than telling a child or adolescent that if he does thus and thus you will react by doing thus and thus, unless you *do* react in that way. What you are doing when you don't follow through is teaching the child that Mom or Dad's word doesn't really mean a thing. For your child's sake, think before you threaten. If major decisions need to be made, sleep on them a night or two and talk about them with your spouse before the two of you approach your teen-ager to discuss it.

2. Watch Your Expectations

Many times parents unknowingly place unrealistic expectations on their children. Standards need to be realistic. You can't impose super-high expectations for your children and maintain an encouraging situation. We live in a world that is perfectionistic-oriented. We are great at picking out flaws rather than the good in people. If parents join the world and also impose unrealistic expectations on their teenagers, they often push them to the brink.

3. Accept Them Where They Are

It's tough to accept your own child where he is. We don't always have trouble accepting other people's children where they are, but we know how we want our children to be, how we want them to think and act. We don't have to agree with the way our children are, but we do have to communicate that we care for them.

Most parents are extremely good at extinguishing their children's feelings while they are still very young.

But if your child or teenager has feelings or opinions about anything which happen to conflict with yours, try to recognize that he has a right to his feelings, hear him out, accept him as he is, then go on from there. If he is immature in the way he thinks, your understanding him and accepting him anyhow will go a long way toward helping him sort out his feelings. However, he may never totally agree with you.

4. Take Time to Listen

This ties in with accepting your child. If you want a relationship with your child, if you want to still be friends with your child when he becomes a man or she becomes a woman, take time to listen. Listening means that your entire energy is geared toward just trying to hear and feel what your child is trying to tell you. Don't be judgmental because you disagree, and don't spend your listening time preparing what you're going to say when he's finished. Really listen.

5. Respect Their Choices

Another tough assignment for us as parents is to respect our children and their choices.

After all, we know what clothes look best on our children; we know what friends are best for our children; we know what activities our children should engage in—we know everything our children should do, say and be. Now why can't they just submit and let us live their lives?

There were some interesting studies done of elementary-age children who were allowed to eat anything they wanted in a school cafeteria during a month of testing. At the beginning of the month-long experiment the children, of course, pigged out on the desserts, sweets and all the goodies. But as the days marched by they began to swing back to a very traditional and well-balanced diet. Kids love to test us. They are going to selectively like things they know we don't just to see if we will love them even though we disagree with them. They want us to respect their choices. Much rebellion during the teen years comes about because kids want their choices—right or wrong—to be respected. Many parents who had to learn to respect their children's choices say now that the kids are grown they have become more like their mother and father than their parents ever would have hoped or thought.

6. Ask for Forgiveness

Too many parents feel they should never have to ask for forgiveness from their child or teenager because they feel they are better. No way! We're all the same; we all fall short. I've seen what happens when parents go in a humble manner to their child and say, "Hey, forgive me." For us as parents to admit that we were insensitive, cruel, mean, forgetful—whatever—to a teenager really makes us stand tall in their eyes. When we can admit that we blew it, all kinds of avenues open up for our children to share with us.

7. Respect Their Privacy

During the adolescent years, as emotions run high and new sexual feelings run rampant in an adolescent's body, your kids need you to step back and let them have their privacy. It's hard to handle the fact that your little boy or little girl doesn't want to crawl into your lap anymore, or go for a ride in the family car, or do much of anything with the family. You really get the feeling that the kid is only interested in having a bunk at the house and some food on the table to keep him going so he can continue his busy social life, answer the phone constantly and attend to his duties at school. But he's building his independence while still under the shelter of your love and concern. Help him by respecting his privacy.

8. Share Your Feelings

If your adolescent asks you, tell him how you feel. One thing I am so thankful for is that my parents always told me how they felt about things. They told me clearly and succinctly and yet they let me make my decisions about things. To me that's a realistic way of sharing with a teenager. Share clearly how you feel.

That reminds me of the story of a country church that struggled for over a year to buy a new chandelier for the sanctuary. They had a promotional campaign and already had the approval of the committee in charge of church expenditures. But it had to go before the congregation, and for an item as costly as this, 100 percent of the congregation needed to approve it. The chairman of the church stood up and asked for the final vote. It was almost unanimous; one old farmer in the back row voted no. So the chairman called for a revote after a few more words of encouragement. Again the farmer voted no. Finally the chairman queried the old man as to why he was resisting buying the chandelier. The old fellow replied, "There's too many other things this church needs, like a light in the sanctuary."

Speak directly to your kids. Call it as you see it. Don't try to dazzle them.

9. Do the Unexpected

Doing the unexpected can be a very good way of communicating respect to children and teenagers and also of making them accountable for the choices they make. For example, suppose Mom and Dad have asked their teenage son and daughter to get dinner started. Mom and Dad come home, perhaps after working all day, and find the dirty breakfast dishes still in the sink and nothing started for dinner. Where are the teenagers? Watching late afternoon television. What do we as parents usually do? Most of us go in, ranting and raving about how undependable those kids are, and stomp around the house creating ill feelings. Then to add fuel to the fire, Mom and Dad go into the kitchen, roll up their sleeves and proceed to clean up and prepare dinner, letting the children off the hook.

I contend that a good way to handle the situation might be for Mom and Dad to simply turn around and leave the house, go out to dinner by themselves and make an evening of it. I would repeat that procedure until such time as the children did as they were told to do. Now, you say, that might be expensive and inconvenient. But isn't it a nice way to have dinner with your husband or wife without the teenagers around?

The point is, we need to hold children responsible for what we expect of them. That's our responsibility as parents. We can't beat them over the heads and make them do things, but neither can we play into their hands. So doing the unexpected sometimes can really be effective.

10. Talk About Potential Problems

It is really important to talk to your children about some of the pitfalls and challenges that lie before them. Again, here is an opportunity to share with them from your own life. Whenever we do that we open good avenues of communication. Talking to a 13- or 14-year-old about when he begins dating at 16 is, in my opinion, a good thing to do. Such communication gives your child time to prepare and will help him or her make rational decisions and be better prepared for many things that can happen. Also the teenager will be more receptive to you when you talk about problems before he has to meet them. The day before the first date is much too late.

11. Don't Act Like a Teenager

It's a temptation for many of us to feel that by not acting our age, we identify with our youngsters and make them feel comfortable with us. Actually the reverse is true. Kids who have parents that try to act, look and talk like teenagers tell me that they feel very self-conscious and embarrassed when their moms or dads attempt to be teenagers. Most adolescents want us as parents to act, look and talk like parents. That's our role. They have plenty of buddies; they need parents. There is a difference.

12. Give Them Choices; Let Them Fail

A tough assignment is to give your children choices

and let them fail. Those of us who feel that we have to control situations in other people find it particularly difficult to give our children choices. There's something anti-American about letting people fail. Yet think about the time when your life turned around, when you began to put things together. Did that experience come out of success or out of failure? If you're like most of us, the good, dramatic changes came out of failure.

Giving a teenager, for example, the choice of mowing the lawn or paying someone else to mow it for him is a good technique. It says, "Hey, you have a choice. Do you want the privilege of paying someone else to do it for you, or to do it yourself?" This method gets our teenagers a little closer to life's realities. As an adult who likes to drive a clean car, I have a choice: should I clean it myself or be lazy and pay four bucks at the carwash? See, life's training ground has to be similar to what real life is all about. There are real responsibilities in the world and kids have to learn how to handle them while they're still in the home. It's the safest place in the world to learn about the realities of life.

13. Don't Snowplow Their School Road

Don't interfere in your child's or adolescent's school life to the point where you take away his incentive and sense of responsibility for his own education. What? Stay out of their school life when just last week the president of the PTA made a speech about parents and children working together to help expand the mind of today's youth? I'm telling you that when you get involved in a kid's school work and activities, 90 percent of the time that involvement is negative involvement. It's important that teenagers learn early in their childhood that their education is their own responsibility and no one else's; and they are going to be held accountable for what they do with the opportunity.

Actually, even kindergartners don't want their parents to be too obvious around their school. One mother I know was going on a field trip with her son's kindergarten class. The little boy said, "Please don't sit near me." Children want their school life separate from their home life.

This is not to say that parents should not give a child encouragement in his homework, or that they shouldn't see to it that he sets aside time to do his homework; but parents should resist the temptation to help him with it or do it for him or try in any way to make it easier for him.

Parents also ought to see to it that the schools encourage responsibility in their children. I recently worked with a family who literally had to beat on the high school principal's desk to get him to flunk their freshman son. All the boy's grades for the entire year were *D*s and *F*s. The kid wasn't learning according to the school's own report system. Yet the school authorities had the audacity to say they were going to promote him to the next grade because they thought it would be bad for him to stay back with the younger children.

Now how are we ever going to teach accountability and responsibility training to children when our system tells them that no matter what they do and how badly they fail, they'll pass anyway? "Don't worry, you'll still get to go through graduation—wear the funny cap and gown, sing a few songs and go to the party with the rest of the guys." Now, that's crazy!

14. Neither Show Them Off Nor Embarrass Them

Every family has at least one kid who's talented, clever, cute, or outstanding in some way. Some people have a whole houseful of kids like that. But, please, spare the kids—and your friends; don't embarrass the kids by making them show off.

It's easy to fall into the trap of showing off your children. Sure you're proud of their accomplishments, whatever they are. But to ask your talented son or daughter to perform for your friends or relatives without first preparing them is putting them on the spot. You wouldn't like someone to put you on the spot that way. Why would you do that to your teenager?

The other side of this is don't embarrass them. When your teenagers goof up, when they don't do the job they were supposed to have done, it's very tempting to browbeat them in front of their peers. How would you feel if someone did that to you? You wouldn't want to be ridiculed or laughed at before your peers by someone you love. So have the courtesy to wait until you're alone with your teenager; then if he needs chewing out, fine! A good chewing out never hurts. Tell him exactly how you feel about things.

15. Don't Be a Flaw-Picker

Traveling right along with embarrassing them is the problem of flaw-picking. Teens see enough flaws in themselves and they magnify their own faults. They don't need their parents pouncing on every little thing they do. Their self-concept is usually at an all-time low during adolescence. Many times it is low because their parents began to whittle away at it while they were very young; the first time your little one made his own bed did Mom come along behind him and remake it, showing him that he didn't do it right? Or when little Johnny helped to clean up the yard, did Dad show him how much he missed rather than how much he helped?

Children and adolescents need to be reminded, coaxed and encouraged to do what they should. They don't need to have someone constantly point out their weaknesses, failures and flaws.

16. Don't Spit in Their Soup

You know what "spit in their soup" is? That's when your daughter asks if she can go to some activity at school that night, and you reply, "Okay, go on along, honey, and have a good time. But you know how I am when you're out at night." See, the "spit in their soup" part is the little something you add at the end of the sentence that says, "Go ahead and go, but you won't have a good time because you know I'm going to be here at home worrying about you." Spitting in the soup is a sure way to create the guilties in your children and create a divisive relationship between you and your son or daughter.

Another thing we as parents do is dig up old bones. It's so easy to go back and remind a teenager about his spotty attendance at school or church, or pull some other little indiscretions out of the past which he has done or hasn't done. Digging up old bones is never instructive, it's usually destructive. Parents, think before you open your mouths.

17. Don't Talk in Volumes

Parents have a way of overdoing things. If your adolescent asks what time it is, tell him what time it is. Don't tell him how Big Ben was made and how it's maintained. Many of us just wait for an opening as innocent as "What time is it?" to bring down volumes of advice and instructions. If you talk in volumes your adolescent will tune you out immediately. Don't ever begin, "When I was your age . . . . " It guarantees an immediate adolescent deafness.

18. Share Your Real Self

Be brave and share with your adolescent your real thoughts and feelings about yourself. You'll pave the way for honest, open communication between you. This is a difficult thing to do because many times we honestly don't want our children to know that we have another side to our lives. But who doesn't have some dark side in his past? Not one of us on this earth. We all have some skeletons in our closet that we're ashamed of and don't feel good about.

Now some of you are thinking, "Why parade that dirty linen in front of our own children?" Well, I think a lot of comfort and encouragement can be given to a child or adolescent when he sees that his parents are human—that they do make mistakes.

Try this exercise for what it's worth. Maybe after dinner some night have each person list on a piece of paper all the attributes and characteristics he or she wants others to think he or she has. Portray the image you project to others. Then on the other side list the qualities and weaknesses you know you have in your real selves. Now exchange papers—parents with kids. This exercise might generate some interesting discussion. As you explain why you said what you said about yourself, take the opportunity to tell some funny, amusing or even dumb stories about your childhood and adolescent years.

19. Don't Praise Your Adolescent

Okay, I realize that most of us grew up feeling that praise was important. In fact, I've seen bumper stickers that say, "Look for the good and praise it." It sounds great, but I've found that praise can be a very defeating thing for your adolescent. How do you feel when someone praises you? I feel very uneasy. I feel that there's a hitch in it somewhere.

You say, "Yes, but how about the people who work for praise?" How about them? I know there are people who look for carrots every time they turn a corner. They constantly need someone stroking them. Fine, but what happens when there isn't someone around to stroke them constantly? What happens when your child or adolescent becomes an adult and can't find a substitute mother or dad to give them strokes? They fall apart. They don't handle things well when they're not praised or stroked.

What is a good substitute for praise? Encouragement is an excellent substitute for praise. The difference is subtle. For example, you come home and find that your son or daughter has surprised you by cleaning up the kitchen. In disbelief you yell for your 13-year-old, Festus. "Festus, come here. Mom loves you. What a great job you did on this kitchen. Here's five dollars."

Can you predict what happens next? The very next day Festus is going to say, "Hey, Mom, where's my five dollars?"

"What five dollars?"

"The five dollars for today."

"Whatta you mean?"

"Well, yesterday you gave me five dollars for cleaning up. So where's my five dollars for today?"

That's the kind of system you create if you go into a relationship with your adolescent based on praise.

The same situation: "Festus, come here. It's a joy to come home and see a clean, sparkling kitchen. So neat! I just want you to know I appreciate your effort so much." Give son a hug. What does that communicate? It communicates to him that Mom noticed what he did and she appreciates his effort. But notice that the emphasis is on his *effort* and not on the *job* he did.

The danger in praising a child or adolescent is that he might view himself as being loved or prized or appreciated because he did the dishes, and that isn't true. We love our adolescents regardless of whether or not they do extra work. Encouragement is far better than praise.

20. Don't Make Mountains Out of Molehills

We find it all too easy to be overly critical with adolescents. When iced tea is spilled at the dinner table your child doesn't need a tirade or a tantrum or a lecture. He just needs to clean it up. Many parents act like it's the beginning of World War III when their kids do one thing wrong.

What do you say when your son hands you his report card and he has three *A*'s and one *C*? Do you get red in the face, grab your throat and scream, "Oh, no! A C! What's with this C?" It would be a lot better to say, "Three A's and a C! I'm really glad to see you enjoy learning. I'll bet you're proud of your effort."

Chances are your teenager will fall right over on the floor out of sheer amazement. Think about that for a second. Three superior efforts and only one average. That's really a neat report card. But many of us feel compelled to go to the C and respond to it rather than to the three A's.

Handling Those Inevitable Hassles

With an adolescent in the home there are going to be conflicts. When a hassle develops and you're feeling that uneasiness between yourself and your adolescent, approach the situation with a positive attitude. Pick a time and a place to discuss the problem where both of you are comfortable and can do so without interruption.

First, give your teenager the opportunity to tell his side of things. Begin by saying, "Robert, I'm very interested in what your feelings were and your reasons for throwing your younger brother into the creek." After your adolescent describes his feelings or reasons, take time to reflect back on what you hear. Give him a chance to clarify so that you understand exactly what he's trying to say.

Next, ask him to listen to your point of view. Again, remember while you are listening to him you aren't thinking of what you are going to say; you are just concentrating on listening. When you give your side, try to be as specific as you can about why you're bothered by the problem. Don't be general. If you're general you're going to leave room for misinterpretation and inaccuracy. Take time to discuss how you would have liked to see the problem handled if you could turn the clock back—which you can't. Then give your adolescent the opportunity to tell how he should have handled the problem.

Lastly, work toward a mutual solution to the problem. That's why you and your teenager sat down and talked about the problem to begin with, so that you could come to an agreeable solution. There might have to be some compromise or some negotiation, but that's true of almost everything in life. If there is some doubt in your mind or your adolescent's mind as to what is expected, take the time to write out the agreement and sign it. Then if there's a need to go back and refer to it, everyone knows exactly what was expected.

I hope these guidelines are useful to you as you go through the teen years with your adolescent. Being a teenager or being a parent of a teenager is not a very easy task and it requires a great amount of determination and willingness to cooperate, as well as much love and understanding to survive those adolescent years.

Chapter 7

Drinking and Drugs Are Dangerous

I recently worked with a young high school senior who had gone to a party at the university while visiting a girlfriend. Of course she had a great need to be just like everybody else, so she walked around with a drink in her hand, sipping it. As many new drinkers do, she guzzled a bit too much too quickly and passed out at the party. Some gentlemen, who were obviously concerned for her welfare, thought enough of her to take her to their apartment. There they removed her clothing and, as best as we could determine, about 10 young men gang-raped this 17-year-old high school student.

Several hours later when she woke up all she had were some faint, frightening memories of what had transpired. What an ugly blemish and memory this young girl has to face. Why? Because she acted irresponsibly. She went along with the crowd and didn't use her head.

Tragedies of Widespread Alcohol Abuse

It's a sad commentary, but drinking totally permeates our society. When someone asks you out for a drink, that doesn't mean a Coke or a cup of coffee, does it? It means an alcoholic beverage. The leading drug problem we have in the United States is that of alcohol. We don't like to think of alcohol as a drug, but it is, and it is having a devastating effect on millions of lives each day.

Ninety-three percent of our high school students have tried alcohol and as many as six percent drink daily.[1] One study concluded that one-third of the country's high school students are problem drinkers; that is, they have gotten drunk more than six times in the past year.[2] Nearly one out of six young people in the tenth to twelfth grades call themselves "heavy drinkers."[3] The nation's single greatest killer of people between 15 and 24 is drunk-driving crashes.[4] Between 1970 and 1980 alone, more than 250,000 Americans have died because of drunk drivers, which is more than four times the number of Americans killed during the 10 years of fighting in the Vietnam war.[5] These facts should be enough to encourage us parents to warn our children against the dangers of drinking alcohol. But there's more.

Doctors Raymond B. Johnson and William Lukash, in a booklet, *Medical Complications of Alcohol Abuse*, say that "alcohol can be a catalyst for violence of all types. There are at least 100,000 alcohol related deaths in the United States each year: 50 percent of the homicides in the United States are alcohol related and 50 percent of all the felons in federal penitentiaries have alcohol related problems. One-third of the suicide victims in this country show significant alcohol intoxication."[6]

Starting Young

Claire Costales, author of *Staying Dry*, says that she became an alcoholic at 17. She began drinking at home—she was born and reared in Ireland—by sneaking drinks at parties in her own home or at parties in friends' homes, which she attended with her family. Claire says that "if booze hadn't been presented to me as acceptable, helpful and glamorous, chances are I would not have chosen a career in alcoholism."[7]

This tells me that the burden of informing—modeling as well as teaching—our children about this great threat to their happiness, their health, and their very lives is on us, their parents. Remember that children and adolescents copy what is modeled for them, and the earliest modeling they have is in the home. If very young children see one or both parents socializing over liquor, offering it to their guests, they will of course assume that's the proper way to act.

At the same time, however, you are telling your child that liquor is not good for him; he has to wait until he's 21 to drink (or 18, 19, or "older"). What does this do? It's like showing him a taste of good things to come, just as that vitally important symbol of adulthood, the car, is. So when that child becomes an adolescent and wants to impress his peers and be "grown up," he takes up social drinking. He hasn't been prepared in his home for the dynamite effect of alcohol (schools and churches make some feeble attempts at education), so the first time he or she drinks at a party it could end up disastrously.

Again I must remind you, begin talking about the danger of the drug alcohol to your children when they are very young. Reinforce the information all the time they are growing up. Keep the avenues of communication open between you so that your adolescent can share with you some of the stories and incidents he becomes aware of at school. Then pay attention to his life-style. In one chapter I urged you to respect your child's privacy, but we also are obligated to be very observant and attentive to his day-by-day activities.

Be Alert

Professionals who work with teenage problem drinkers suggest a number of areas where parents should be alert. Among them are: know if your teenagers are attending school each day or not; see if they are defensive when questioned about alcohol; be aware of behavioral changes such as extreme boredom, moodiness or exhaustion; know where they're going and with whom; be present if they have a party at your house; if they ever get into a situation where they have had too much to drink, and they call you to come pick them up, do so without recriminations.

If you should ever happen to find your teenager drunk, take care of his immediate needs, and then get him to bed. The next day, while his head is still pounding from the night before, be direct and straightforward with him about what happened.

Worse for Women

I've used the generic "he" as I've described what to do with the teenage drinker, but alcohol abuse is also a growing problem among women. According to Dr. Eleanor Hanna, Director of the Alcohol Clinic of Massachusetts General Hospital, "The cocktail party is replacing the tea party for many women. The so-called 'two-martini lunch' is no myth. There is a total naiveté among many female patients who come to our clinic about their physiological inability to tolerate as much alcohol as a man."[8]

Now here's one good reason why young women need to realize that there really are significant differences between men and women. As Dr. Hanna points out, men are apparently able to maintain a constant level of tolerance to alcohol, but the level women can tolerate varies greatly. This could be due to the menstrual cycle and the use of contraceptives. So drinking alcohol, as in most other areas, is a greater threat and danger to the female than it is to the male.

How Can You Know?

Maybe your adolescent, or someone else's son or daughter, is already having an alcohol problem. Perhaps you are thinking, "Oh, a few beers once in a while aren't going to hurt." But maybe your child is one who can't take a few beers once in a while and leave it alone. Claire Costales points out in her book, *Staying Dry*, that "medical experts now believe that the tendency to alcoholism is hereditary; that there is a genetic differentiation between people who drink and become addicted and those who drink and do not."[9]

How can your teenager know if alcohol is a problem for him? He can't until it's almost too late and he becomes an alcoholic. Alcoholics Anonymous distributes a sheet prepared by Johns Hopkins University Hospital that is a self-test to determine if someone is an alcoholic.

The questions must be answered as honestly as possible.

1. Do you lose time from work (or school) due to drinking?

2. Is drinking making your home life unhappy?

3. Do you drink because you are shy with other people?

4. Is drinking affecting your reputation?

5. Have you ever felt remorse after drinking?

6. Have you gotten into financial difficulties as a result of drinking?

7. Do you turn to lower companions and an inferior environment when drinking?

8. Does your drinking make you careless of your family's welfare?

9. Has your ambition decreased since drinking?

10. Do you crave a drink at a definite time daily?

11. Do you want a drink the next morning?

12. Does drinking cause you to have difficulty in sleeping?

13. Has your efficiency decreased since drinking?

14. Is drinking jeopardizing your job or business (or school work)?

15. Do you drink to escape from worries or trouble?

16. Do you drink alone?

17. Have you ever had a complete loss of memory as a result of drinking?

18. Has your doctor ever treated you for drinking?

19. Do you drink to build up your self-confidence?

20. Have you ever been to a hospital or institution on account of drinking?

A yes to any one of these questions is a definite warning that the person taking the test may be an alcoholic. Two yes answers indicate the test-taker probably is an alcoholic. If the person taking the test answered yes to three or more questions and wants to stop drinking, he or she should call the local office of AA, or write to Alcoholics Anonymous, P. O. Box 459, Grand Central Station, New York, NY 10017.

Other Drug Problems

Alcohol is the most abused drug in the United States, the number one drug problem among teenagers. The number two abuse is tobacco and number three is marijuana. Following is more from Chuck's tape transcript. You remember we quoted him in an earlier chapter.

"Hello. My name is Chuck and I thought I'd talk to you about some of the experiences I've had with drugs in the past. I'm 25 years old. I graduated from high school in 1975.

"I started getting high on drugs when I was a freshman in high school. I guess if you were to ask me why I started getting high I'd say it was probably because everybody was doing it, it was the thing to do, and you weren't cool if you weren't doing it. Before I let peer pressure take over I used to enjoy telling people that I didn't get high or drink and didn't smoke cigarettes. I can still say truthfully that I've never smoked a whole cigarette—and don't guess I've taken five hits off a cigarette in my whole life. But with dope you weren't cool if you didn't participate.

"I have to admit the first couple of times I tried pot I didn't get too much out of it, but I kept on doing it and kept on doing it until it got to be where it was a fun thing to do. I'd go to parties and at first I'd really laugh a lot and it was just a good time. My friends and I would get giggly and all that stuff. The first couple of months it was a lot of fun—it was a cool thing to do. Instead of going to class we'd go out and catch a 'buzz.' When we came back everybody saw we had red eyes and thought we were cool. So it was really neat to walk into class and let everybody know we were high. You know how everybody does, they walk up to you and talk so they blow their breath on you to let you know they were out getting high at lunch. That's pretty cool if you think about it.

"It wasn't till a couple of years later that I really started having bad feelings about marijuana—I wasn't smart enough to see what it was doing to me but I could sure see what it was doing to my friends. It seemed that a lot of procrastination was happening in their lives. We'd get high in the morning and just kind of waste the day, just breeze through the whole day, not really accomplishing anything, just lay there and watch TV, go play ball or do nothing. And you can't really live today tomorrow. I really feel strongly that you should accomplish something, whether it's learning something, bettering yourself physically or mentally or whatever. Inside I didn't feel good about just sitting around all day and not doing anything. And that was pretty common with marijuana."

Chuck found out what many scientists and physicians have now proved, that marijuana creates a particular personality in its users. In some people the effects do not show up for several years; in others the personality impairment is almost immediate. These distinct traits are called "pot personality" symptoms: impaired short-term memory; emotional flatness; the dropout syndrome— out of sports, out of school, out of family; diminished willpower, concentration, attention span, ability to deal with abstract or complex problems, and tolerance for frustration; increased confusion in thinking, impaired judgment, hostility toward authority.[10]

More than four million children between the ages of 12 and 17 smoke marijuana regularly (these are 1979 statistics) and the figures are still rising.[11] Denise Kendel, in one study, points out the tremendous power of peer pressure among adolescents. She said that those teenagers whose friends use illegal drugs are also more likely to use drugs themselves.[12]

What Can Parents Do?

Of all the studies I have reviewed regarding the use of drugs by adolescents, one really hits the nail on the head. An article by Cynthia G. Tudor, David M. Petersen and Kirk W. Elifson tells that studies show that the *closer* the adolescent is to his or her parents, the *less likely* that he or she will use drugs. The more *independent* the adolescent is from his parents, the *greater the likelihood* that he will use drugs.[13] That really says something, doesn't it?

If you're not taking the time to talk to your children about drugs, you'd better start. Drugs are as accessible to children and adolescents today as Hershey bars were available to us. Talk to your kids about drugs, about the values you want them to have. If you're a believer, show them what God's Word says about defiling your body. Show them the articles in the newspapers about people dying because of alcohol and drug abuse. (The classic examples are the recent deaths of promising young sports stars, deaths that were directly caused by drug abuse.)

It's amazing to me the number of kids I see who seem to be determined to do themselves in. Several years ago it was my unfortunate task to call a mom and dad in the midwest and notify them that their son had overdosed. You see, he didn't pay much attention to what many professionals have tried to explain, that the combination of booze and drugs is a deadly one. This young man had several beers and then popped some barbiturates. Early in the morning his roommate returned from his night on the town and noticed something very peculiar about this young man—his neck was blue. He was dead. A 19-year-old's life was snuffed out because he was irresponsible. I'd be willing to bet that his parents never took the time to talk with their son about the deadly nature of drugs.

Perhaps those parents didn't know where to begin or didn't have the necessary information. There's no excuse for that today. Every community has all kinds of information about drug use. Ask your family doctor or the local community health service or the police department or your public library.

How do you begin to talk to your adolescent or child about drugs? First, let him know you really care about him as a person and would like to know how he feels about drug use. If teenagers see that their parents want to be close to them and really do love them, chances are they will open up, share their thoughts and be responsive to what their parents want to teach them. These are the kids who probably will not get involved with drugs.

I know it's scary. One thing I hear parents say continually is, "I worry about my kid and alcohol and driving the car, getting stoned, doing something that's totally irresponsible and out of character." Why do they do things that are irresponsible and totally out of character? The answer is, when they're stoned or so wasted they can't see straight, they are not able to respond as they would otherwise. When do many young girls experience first sex? When they're so stoned or smashed they can't think clearly and can't remember the next day exactly what happened.

Help Them Make the Right Choice

The reality of the eighties is that drugs are easily available. Your kids are going to have to make a choice whether or not they will use drugs. They are going to have to have the courage of their convictions to say, "No, I don't want to be like everyone else and just follow along." But they need your help.

Most of us have heard the story of Carol Burnett's life, how both her parents were alcoholics and the only stabilizing factor in her life was her grandmother, who really showed that she loved Carol.

Carrie, Carol's own daughter, started using drugs at age 13. By the time Carrie reached 14 Carol became aware of her daughter's intense drug problem and put her in a hospital. In an interview she was asked if she blamed herself for her daughter's problem with drugs. Miss Burnett answered, "I did at first." Then she realized that her daughter was trying to cop out with the excuse that she took drugs because her mother was famous, and she too was thrust into the limelight and couldn't handle it.

Carol said, "Tell me, who lives a normal life? I never did! I would rather my parents had been me and I had lived the kind of life my kids have than to have grown up as I did. Everybody is born with something they have to overcome." Then she said something I think is very significant. "It's their [the kids'] responsibility [to take charge of their own lives]. I had to deal with my parents—I don't blame them. I did what I could with myself. All kids have to do the same . . . . Everybody finds something to complain about—that's human nature. But we are all responsible for ourselves."[14]

How true! We are all responsible for ourselves. But parents are responsible for teaching their kids to be responsible.

If you've never taken time to talk to your children about booze, drugs and sex, perhaps today would be a good day to start. Some parents are uncomfortable talking about these subjects with their kids. That's probably because their parents didn't talk to them. Here is a suggestion that might make it easier. Take your children, one at a time, away somewhere overnight or for a weekend—a combination fun and serious-talking time. While you're in the car driving to your weekend spot, when you can't look at each other eyeball to eyeball, begin to open up. Talk turkey about the subjects you've been avoiding. There's something magic about frank discussions with others while you're out driving.

When younger children ask about sex or drugs or alcohol, be candid with them. Take time to explain. Be relevant and not too wordy. Answer their questions seriously, frankly and without embarrassment. Don't put them down in any shape or form. You, the parent, have to be the most reliable source of information for your child.[15]

Chapter 8

You Are Something Special

This is an open letter to your adolescents. Encourage them to read it. Better yet, read and discuss it with them.

Take a look around you. Don't you feel like most people are happier than you are? As I said to your parents earlier in this book, adolescence is a time when things are exaggerated—when other people really do seem better off than you. That feeling is only natural due to the great amount of insecurity and uncertainness an adolescent has.

Think about Mom and Dad for a moment. It's hard to believe that at one time in their lives they also felt ugly, unwanted, rejected and insecure. If Mom and Dad have followed the suggestions I've made in this book, they have already shared with you about the real self-images and thoughts they had about themselves when they were growing up.

Changing Relationships and Values

Of course, what's of prime importance to most teen-agers are those very special relationships they form during high school days—not only with friends of the opposite sex, but friends of the same sex as well. Once your high school days are ended, however, as hard as it will be for you to believe now, those relationships will basically end. There will be a fracturing of the friends whom you now think will be your lifetime buddies. All of a sudden they'll vanish as they leave your community and go away to school, take jobs in various parts of the country or get married. The whole gang just sort of vanishes into thin air. You'll be lucky to see some of them at 10-year intervals at the old high school reunion.

Speaking of that 10-year high school reunion, it may seem like a million years off, but you really have a choice to make right now. How do you want to be seen at that high school reunion when you walk in there with your husband or wife? Do you want to meet previous lovers eyeball-to-eyeball? Or do you want to walk into a room where there are many people with whom you've had good times, without any skeletons in your closet? You don't have to look into anybody's eyes who will make you feel guilty or angry or hurt or any of those things—at least not as a direct result of sexual activity with them.

Your big advantage right now as a teenager is to realize that your virginity is yours, and there's nothing wrong with wanting to preserve yourself for marriage. The fact remains that once you fork it over, you can't retrieve it. You really have to decide that right now. Do you want sex to be really special and sacred and something to look forward to? Or do you want to be like so many other kids your age who have too much too fast? Do you want to have sex become something dirty, nasty, a guilt-ridden experience for you in life?

I think you probably realize that the years ahead are going to mean many changes for you. Right now you might judge a restaurant by whether or not it has video machines in the lobby. But 10 years from now you may be more impressed by their béarnaise sauce. All of us, whether we like to admit it or not, are going to do a lot of changing between graduation and the first high school reunion. Take pride in the fact that you are special and different and not like anybody else.

Much to Look Forward To

So as you approach adulthood and freedom and independence, I hope you do it with optimism and with a great deal of excitement, because there is an awful lot in life to enjoy and benefit from.

Of course many new experiences are exciting in the young person's life, but there are a lot of scary ones too. The good news is that at the end of this long dark tunnel called adolescence there is a world that can be what you want it to be, a world where you can be happy and have self-worth and an opportunity to accomplish some of the things you'd like to in life. Adolescence isn't forever, thank goodness! Things have to get better, don't they? Can you believe that there will be a time in your life when pimples will become a thing of the past? That's reason enough to celebrate in itself.

Birds of a Feather

Someone once said that "birds of a feather flock

together." I think there's an awful lot of truth in that statement.

If you really are concerned about a good reputation, then be selective about whom you run with and associate with. I realize there is an awful lot of pressure to be like everybody else. You know, 30 years ago if somebody smoked pot or engaged in sex rather casually, people were really surprised. Most people were offended. The tragic thing today is that it's now reversed; if you don't go along with the group and smoke dope and be like everybody else, people have a hard time believing that you don't.

Building Strength

There are going to be temptations, and you can't rely on Mom and Dad alone as you deal with these situations face-to-face, one-on-one. You're going to have to build your own strength and courage to say no to things you know aren't good for you. As you approach major decisions in your life, move slowly on those decisions. Realize that there's a normal part of your life right now that seems to insist that everything has to be done immediately, but fight that tendency with conscious, rational thought. Decisions don't always have to be made immediately. Sleep on them and think about them. Talk about them with your best friend or your parents. In some cases your best friends might really be your parents; maybe you have the kind of relationship where you can talk with them about anything. I hope so.

We Need Each Other

I also hope this book has helped both you and your

parents to be able to talk on an honest level, taking off the many masks we all wear. As one 15-year-old girl said, "Boy, if my mom and dad knew what I did they'd die." They probably wouldn't die; they'd probably understand. They've probably been through some of the same trials and tribulations you're going through right now.

A final note: Realize and accept the fact that, like everyone else, you are imperfect and need others in your life. I know you like to be cool as an adolescent and to act like you don't have a worry in the world. But those of us who work with adolescents daily know that there are plenty of worries in the world of the adolescent. You have to realize that if you try to shoulder all of those worries yourself, it's going to be a long, tough road. It might even be an impossible road. Share your thoughts and your burdens with your parents. Share your burdens with your heavenly Father. Ask and seek direction in your life.

God thinks you are very special. You're so special that He even knows the number of hairs on your head. It's hard to believe, but it's true. He says He'll meet your every need; what does that mean? Every sexual need? Of course He's going to meet those sexual needs. How? By bringing someone very special to you to be your life's partner. If you seek God's direction someday someone very special will enter your life. If you have the courage to wait you heighten the probability of having that one special person come in and share the joys and pleasures and rewards of this life with you.

May the rocky road of your adolescent years be tolerable, and provide you with great learning experiences that will reinforce your understanding of real love.

You are something special—very special. Don't ever put yourself in a position where you are used by someone or where you are using someone else. People are for loving, not for using.

A Teenager's Ten Commandments to Parents

1. Please don't give me everything I say I want. Saying no shows me you care. I appreciate guidelines.
2. Don't treat me as a little kid. Even though you know what's "right," I need to discover some things for myself.
3. Respect my need for privacy. Often I need to be alone to sort things out and daydream.
4. Never say, "In my day . . . " That's an immediate turn off. Besides, the pressures and responsibilities of my world are more complicated.
5. I don't pick your friends or clothes, please don't criticize mine. We can disagree and still respect each other's choices.
6. Refrain from always rescuing me; I learn most from my mistakes. Hold me accountable for the decisions I make in life, it's the only way I'll learn to be responsible.
7. Be brave enough to share your disappointments, thoughts and feelings with me. I'm never too old to be told I'm loved.
8. Don't talk in volumes. I've had years of good instruction, now trust me with the wisdom you have shared.
9. I respect you when you ask me for forgiveness for a thoughtless deed on your part. It proves that neither of us is perfect.
10. Set a good example for me as God intended you to do; I pay more attention to your actions than your words.

For information regarding speaking engagements or seminars, write or call:

Dr. Kevin Leman
1325 N. Wilmot Rd.
Suite 320
Tucson, AZ 85712
(602) 886-9925

Notes

Introduction
1. Ronald L. Koteskey, "Growing Up Too Late Too Soon," *Christianity Today*, March 13, 1981, p. 24.

Chapter One
1. James Dobson, *Preparing for Adolescence* (Ventura, CA: Vision House Publishers, 1978).
2. Koteskey, "Growing Up Too Late Too Soon," p. 24.
3. Dobson, *Preparing for Adolescence.*

Chapter Two
1. Ibid.
2. Carol Greenberg Felsenthal, "Teen Suicide—What to Do When a Friend Is in Trouble," *Seventeen,* April 1979, pp. 184, 185.
3. Suicide Prevention Service, Ventura, California.
4. Patrick C. McHenry, Carl L. Tishler, Karen L. Christman, "Adolescent Suicide and the Classroom Teacher," *The Education Digest,* September 1980, pp. 43-45.

Chapter Three
1. "Did He Leave You with More Than a Memory?" *Mademoiselle,* August 1980, p. 106.
2. Midge Lasky Schildkraut, "The Startling New Facts About VD," *Good Housekeeping,* September 1979, pp. 227, 228.
3. "Herpes: New VD in Town," *MS.*, December 1980, p. 62.
4. Center for Disease Control, Atlanta, Georgia.

5. Scott Kraft, "Unwed Mothers List Fears of Rushing into Marriage," *Santa Barbara News Press,* November 26, 1981, p. C1.
6. Alan Guttmacher Institute as quoted in *People,* May 4, 1981, pp. 56-60.
7. "Teenage Birth Control," *Society,* March/April 1979, p. 3.
8. Dick Pawelek, "Study Shows That Teens Lack Knowledge of Pregnancy Risk," *Senior Scholastic,* November 15, 1979, p. 22.
9. Dr. Kevin O'Reilly and Dr. Sevgi Aral, "Adolescence and Sexual Behavior," *Journal of Adolescent Care,* 1985.
10. Nancy Evans, "Living Together—Who's Most Likely to Succeed or Fail?" *Glamour,* March 1979, p. 232.

Chapter 4
1. Alan Guttmacher Institute, *People.*
2. Linda L. Hendrixson, "Pregnant Children: A Socio-Educational Challenge," *Phi Delta Kappan,* May 1979, pp. 663, 666.
3. Katherine B. Davis, *Factors in the Sex Life of Twenty-Two Hundred Women* (New York: Arno Press, 1972).
4. Alan Guttmacher Institute, *People.*
5. "Teenage Birth Control," p. 3.
6. Ibid.
7. Ibid.

Chapter 5
1. H. Norman Wright and Marvin Inmon, *Dating, Waiting and Choosing a Mate* (Eugene, OR: Harvest House Publishers, 1978), pp. 145, 146.
2. Ann Landers, "Love and Sex Not the Same," © 1981 Field Newspaper Syndicate and the Tucson Citizen.

Chapter 7
1. Lloyd D. Johnston, Jerald G. Bachman, Patrick M. O'Malley, *Student Drug Use in America 1975-1980* (Washington, D.C.: National Institute on Drug Abuse, 1981).
2. "A Head Start on Drinking," *America,* April 4, 1981, p. 270.
3. Clifford Berman, "Is *Your* Child a Secret Alcoholic?" *Good Housekeeping,* June 1981, pp. 215, 216.
4. *Alcohol Fact Sheet,* Alcohol Control Center, Ventura, California.
5. "Drunk Driving: A License to Kill," *Reader's Digest,* February 1982, p. 80.
6. Raymond B. Johnson and William Lukash, *Medical Complications of Alcohol Abuse,* Summary of 1973 AMA Washington Conference, p. 6.
7. Claire Costales, *Staying Dry* (Ventura, CA: Regal Books, 1980), p. 30.
8. Eleanor Hanna, *Massachusetts General Hospital News,* September 1981.
9. Costales, *Staying Dry,* p. 20.
10. Peggy Mann, "Marijuana Alert III: The Devastation of Personality," *Reader's Digest,* December 1981, p. 81.
11. Marrill Rogers Skrocki, "Marijuana—the Disturbing New Facts," *McCalls,* June 1979, p. 57.
12. Denise B. Kendel, "Homophili, Selection and Socialization in Adolescent

Friendships," *American Journal of Sociology,* September 1978, p. 427.

13. Cynthia G. Tudor, David M. Petersen, and Kirk W. Elifson, "An Examination of the Relationship Between Peer and Parental Influences and Adolescent Drug Use," *Adolescence,* Winter 1980, p. 795.

14. Dotson Rader, "The Triumph of Carol Burnett," *Parade,* January 5, 1982, p. 7.

15. Lloyd V. Allen, Jr., *Drug Abuse* (Ventura, CA: Regal Books, 1981).